Managing Your Metron

A practical theology of work,
mission and meaning

Managing Your Metron: A Practical Theology of Work, Mission and Meaning

Scripture quotations, unless otherwise indicated, are taken from the New American Standard Bible® (NASB), Copyright ©1960, 1962, 1963, 1968, 1971, 1972, 1973,1975, 1977, 1995 by The Lockman Foundation. Used by permission. www.Lockman.org

Scripture taken from the Holy Bible, New International Version®, NIV. Copyright ©1973, 1978, 1984, 2011 by Biblica, Inc.™ Used by permission of Zondervan. All rights reserved worldwide. www.zondervan.com The "NIV" and "New International Version" are trademarks registered in the United States Patent and Trademark Office by Biblica, Inc.™

Scripture taken from the New King James Version®. Copyright © 1982 by Thomas Nelson. Used by permission. All rights reserved.

Scripture taken from The Holy Bible, English Standard Version. ESV® Text Edition: 2016. Copyright © 2001 by Crossway Bibles, a publishing ministry of Good News Publishers.

Scripture taken from the Holy Bible, Contemporary English Version (CEV) Copyright © 1995 by American Bible Society

JONATHAN NOWLEN

MANAGING YOUR

Metron

A practical theology of work, mission and meaning

Contents

Introduction

ALL ASPECTS OF OUR LIVES ON EARTH happen within a God-ordained sphere of influence. In this season of spiritual history, God has designed each of us to co-labor with him to manage what the apostle Paul describes as a "Metron." All aspects of your life and vocation exist in the context of your metron. God has given you tremendous responsibility regardless of who you are or what you do. He has extended to you a commission and a mission, and he has given you an opportunity to shine.

> "The highest heavens belong to the Lord, but the earth he has given to mankind." (Psalm 115:16 NIV)

Did you know that God put you in charge of his creation? Have you ever wondered if your day to day vocation is sacred and of eternal importance? Do you believe that you can shape the world around you? What does God expect from you? How big is your vision in life? Do you feel that there is no way that you can make a difference and that you are somehow stuck in a "secular" occupation? If we are to invest our lives with purpose and power in the Kingdom of God, these questions must be answered. Finding answers to these questions will free you to embrace your calling and thrive in your occupation.

God has given you not only *permission* but a *commission* to work!

This book is intended to put forward a neglected, yet transformational narrative that I believe is clearly visible in Scripture. We will explore a narrative that begins with Adam and Eve and yet defines our purpose in the Kingdom of God today. This is the story of the Original Commission.

I will consider this book a success if it helps you realize your significance in the Kingdom of God. I believe there is a simple understanding of all things that once discovered, changes everything. No matter who you are or the circumstances of your life, every human bears the image of God and carries an original design. This design is intended for the glory of God and the good of all creation.

My hope and prayer for you is that you would gain a kingdom perspective of your God-given occupation. In this book, we will explore a scriptural narrative that will offer a reformational understanding of vocation and the nature of co-laboring with God. This study is intended to help any believer make sense of life through understanding work, mission, and meaning. This work aims to distill a large amount of scriptural truth, its principles, and theological concepts into an accessible framework. This study is a practical theology that aims to provide you with insight into God's framework for mankind.

The framework that I am endeavoring to provide does not give you all the answers and intentionally avoids giving any "how to" specifics. The body of Christ is overflowing with concepts, practices, and thought leadership that provides specific life applications. Scripturally-based action steps and lifestyle guidance are readily available and well developed. This theological framework is intended to provide you with a structure on to which you can attach these practicals. I have found that there are a lot of available materials with which to finish out the house but that a framework structure that would ultimately hold it all together was hard to locate.

My vision for this study is to create a container or context into which all manner of experience, principles, traditions, spiritual disciplines, theology could be added. There needs to be a starting point that enables one to take action in life. One could describe this work as a backdrop that helps focus and frame the primary activity in a stage production. One could also describe this work as a road that enables one's vehicle to reach its destination and yet is not the vehicle itself. As a practical theology, the aim is to enable you to solidly build and manage that to which God has called you.

There are eternal value and expression of God to be found within all the diverse streams and traditions in the Body of Christ. I hope that any Biblically-based expression of the global church will find this practical theology a useful structure on which to build. I believe this Biblical framework is relevant and functional for all ethnicities and cultures in the body of Christ.

Work is eternal in nature and supernatural by design. We serve a supernatural God and live in a supernatural world and work is God's original design for all people. I hope that you find freedom and joy through realizing that your vocation is a deep and supernatural calling from God and that it is not a form of punishment. I believe that God is knowable and he wants to be known. In this book, we are going to take a journey throughout all of scripture, all of history and explore the meaning of life.

There is hope! A full recovery of your purpose and validation of your vocation is possible! Freedom from boredom, apathy, and dissipation can be realized by embracing one's original commission and realizing your original design.

My life has been filled with incredible experiences with God over the last 25 years of service. I assure you that what I am writing about in this book is effective and has changed lives and the destiny of nations. I have helped to build and operate nation transforming enterprises that are structured on the practical theology that I am presenting. This is a theology of action and co-laboring with God. It is not just a theory but has successfully informed mine, and many other efforts to see nations transformed, and the Kingdom of God expanded. It is a practical, practiced and proven theology that empowers you to manage your metron.

I aim to put forward a framework by which everything learned can find a way to be lived. I hope you find this work accessible and actionable. When you finish this study, you will be enabled to know your place in God's kingdom enterprise. Simplicity is the aim and making the complex practical is the vision. As a child of God, you have the right to live as one who knows their value and who understands their purpose. Once you read this book, you will have a stronger context for understanding scripture and life's meaning.

Theologian N.T. Wright offers a compelling perspective on the meaning of life once one has entered the Kingdom of God. In his book titled *Surprised by Hope*, he writes, "What you do in the present — by painting, preaching, singing, sewing, praying, teaching, building hospitals, digging wells, campaigning for justice, writing poems, caring for the needy, loving your neighbor as yourself — will last into God's future. These activities are not simply ways of making the present life a little less beastly, a little more bearable, until the day when we leave it behind altogether. They are part of what we may call building for God's kingdom."[1]

The quest for the meaning of life always drives humankind. This quest stems from God's universal *software-code* embedded in the human soul. God

---

1 *N.T.Wright; Surprised by Hope: Rethinking Heaven, the Resurrection, and the Mission of the Church*

longs to reveal himself to you and give you answers to this quest. He has built into your very design a desire for the divine. This desire can only be fulfilled by relationship with your creator. He left us the official guide to the software written in our souls, the Bible. He also sent those who believe in him the greatest teacher of all, the Holy Spirit. He has made himself knowable and accessible to his people. He wants to be known. All creation was masterfully designed. You were originally designed to be integral, to matter, in God's epic kingdom project.

Historically, even noted and devoted men and women of faith have struggled to find their calling. Purpose is often elusive even in the Kingdom of God. It is no surprise that we might also struggle with the feeling that God's plans for us are hidden. Vaguely we seem to be aware of something pulling at our heart, tugging us in the direction of greatness. This pull says, "You were created for something more."

We have to let the truth of God's nature and character change your perspective if we are to secure our destiny. It is not in his nature to torment you or hold back fulfillment and purpose. His nature is like that of the loving parent who hides Easter eggs for his children. He wants to give you the joy of discovery and the blessing of good gifts. He hides things "for you" not "from you." He wants you to find your purpose. Part of his original design is that you would experience your significance — that you would know he has made you to matter.

No matter the socio-economic or cultural background from which one has emerged, most people have the same desires in life. This commonality of desires, hopes, and dreams unite us as humanity and point towards an inscription of the divine on the hearts of man. Even those who are not yet saved into God's kingdom tend to toward God's design. The creator has left his signature on the hearts and minds of his prize creation. This signature could be described as embedded software code. God has hard-coded software into our very design. This software drives us to figure out who we are, why we are, and how we got here.

For better or worse, this quest motivates much of human endeavor. Regardless of cultural or ethnic background, we as humans know that we are here for a reason. We all know deep inside that we have inherent value, that we matter. This God authored personal software drives the direction and destiny of individuals and nations. God's original design was that this guiding software would drive us towards the arms of our loving father, the one who designed us and who gave value to each human being. The beautiful secret of this quest is that we find our father as we seek answers to these questions.

As followers of Jesus, this software also guides our choices and affects the use of our life energies. When it comes to this universal quest for answers, as Christians, we have the advantage. We have the source code of the software, the Bible, and we have the greatest teacher, the Holy Spirit. We also have personal access to the author of scripture through the redemptive work of Jesus Christ. In addition to the scriptures, the body of Christ has accumulated a vast amount of study, thought, insight, theology, scholarship, and experience. Many current and past followers of Christ have succeeded in providing believers with vital wisdom as a result of their personal, dynamic walk with God. In knowing God, answers are made known.

We are blessed to be able to build on the foundations and experience of those who have gone before us and those who have walked beside us. These amazing men and women of God have unlocked new levels of understanding, and we are indebted to them.

Because I am confident in the character and nature of God, I am confident in his intentions towards his children. He has good gifts for his children! The greatest gift we can receive is reconciliation with God and then the ministry of reconciliation within God's creation. I am confident that as we explore this theology of work, mission, and meaning, we will discover that we truly do matter in God's original design. Be assured the Kingdom of God is advancing, and you live in the greatest spiritual era in human history — the kingdom era.

Chapter 1
Made to Matter

*"Your kingdom come. Your will be done, On earth
as it is in heaven."* (Matthew 6:10)

Is it possible that the prayer Jesus prayed when he taught his disciples to pray, was actually intended to be answered?

Like me, you may have just mentally skipped over this section where Jesus prayed, "...on earth as it is in heaven..." because we have no grid to understand the implications of what he prayed. I have come to understand that this prayer is not as abstract as it may appear at first glance. In fact, as believers and followers of Christ, we are positioned by God to be part of seeing this prayer answered. All of history, all of scripture and the meaning of life are intricately woven into a redemptive narrative that is found in the fulfillment of this prayer. This redemptive narrative is not only designed to bring hope and a future to all people but also to answer the burning fire in every believer's soul that asks the question, "Do I matter"?

Our spirit knows that we were created in the image and likeness of God, and our very nature is hard-wired to connect with our maker. The fact that everyone is born to matter is at the heart of all human existence. Failure in this basic human quest is the root of all of the world's problems. These problems are complex, but the solutions are simple. The world system offers endless counterfeits and temporary alternatives for this quest of the soul. In the end, it bankrupts the life of those it deceives. Like any counterfeit, you eventually realize that it doesn't have value and are often left worse off in the end. When we as humans connect with our heavenly Father we can come to realize our position in God's original design. When we are born again in Christ Jesus, the Bible states that we have become a new life form.

2nd Corinthians 5:17 explains, "Therefore if anyone is in Christ, he is a *new creature*; the old things passed away; behold, new things have come."

You, as a new creature, have been restored to your proper position in God's design for mankind. As one who has been redeemed, you are now seated in heaven yet living on earth.

Colossians 1:13 describes what happens at salvation when the scripture says, "For he rescued us from the domain of darkness, and transferred us to the kingdom of his beloved Son."

You are a multi-dimensional being who has a body but is a spirit. You live in two realms simultaneously and who you are on earth is shaped by where you sit in heaven. This is one of the great mysteries of God's design. The key to effective kingdom living on earth starts with realizing that as a believer, are currently seated with Christ Jesus in heavenly places.

"And God raised us up with Christ and seated us with him in the heavenly realms in Christ Jesus."(Ephesians 2:6)

The Bible says that once we have believed on the Lord, our very nature has been transformed, and we find ourselves living in two realities. On the one hand, we are seated in heavenly places, and on the other, we are solidly standing in the natural world. This makes us *naturally supernatural*. The joy in our earthly journey is that we get to live in the natural world just as we do before the throne of heaven. God has put us into our spheres of influence to be a bridge or conduit that brings the presence and ways of God into creation.

The naturally supernatural follower of Christ is one who maintains an eternal perspective on all that surrounds them. A spiritually-minded believer is familiar with the ways of God and aims to reproduce the culture of Heaven into the sphere of influence that God has given them on earth. The introduction of God's presence and ways into creation is the true definition of transformation and the heart of his original design.

An untold number of philosophical and theological commentaries have attempted to answer the fundamental question many believers ask, "Why are we still here?" A follower of Christ may find themselves asking, "If God is love," as the scripture says in 1 John 4:8, then why does he leave us in this fallen and pain-filled world once we embrace salvation? Wouldn't it be the most loving thing he could do to remove us from this world once we have believed? Many believers will go on to ask, "Is it loving for God to leave his children in this fallen mess to suffer once they have become part of his family?" Since this is often a normal line of questioning for Christians, it is evident that we don't understand that we are not just saved from something, but we are also saved to something.

I would suggest that many believers have a very limited and self-focused understanding of purpose. Thinking that we are only saved from "sin" and the "world" leads one to struggle to understand correctly one's purpose and identity. In the kingdom being saved *from* is also being saved *to*. The identity of the believer in Christ is defined by who God says we are and that he declares we are seated with Christ Jesus in heavenly places. (Ephesians 2:6) Now that we are redeemed through salvation into God's family, we discover that we have co-inherited all things with Christ Jesus.

> *"The Spirit himself testifies with our spirit that we are children of God, and if children, heirs also, heirs of God and fellow heirs with Christ."* (Romans 8:16–17b)

According to the scripture, we are co-heirs with Christ in the Kingdom of God. This is a huge enhancement to our understanding of reality and raises not a few questions. One of these being, "What shall I do with this inheritance?"

> *"Therefore if anyone is in Christ, he is a **new creature**; the old things passed away; behold, new things have come."* (2 Corinthians 5:17)

Let's start by looking at what happens when you receive Christ and are born again. You become a new creature, and the old "you" has passed away. You are transformed from a sinner who wants to be a saint into a saint who might still choose to sin. Salvation gives you a new identity. As one who is born again, you receive dual citizenship and begin to manage a multi-dimensional identity. Your spiritual passport indicates that you are a citizen of heaven and a citizen of earth. Your spiritual birth certificate indicates that not only are you a dual citizen, but your father is the King and the creator of heaven and earth. You are always in his domain and under his jurisdiction. When we realize who we are as God's children, confidence flows from our lives, and there is no place for fear. Our identity rests on what God declares over us. What he says is true is, indeed, what is true.

When you are transferred into the Kingdom of God through faith in Christ, you are not only saved from judgment, but a whole new identity is imparted to you. The good news is that you are saved from sin, and you have been given a new nature. The software of your soul has been rewritten. As one who is co-inheriting with Christ, you have been enfranchised. Scripture declares that the new creature you have become gives you a place in God's house. And as such you have become a fellow heir with Christ, and you are a rightful heir to what also belongs to Christ. What belongs to Christ?

> *"And he put **all things** in subjection under his feet, and gave him as head over all things to the church, which is his body, the fullness of **him who fills all in all.**"* (Ephesians 1:22–23)

You have inherited the Kingdom of God, but that inheritance comes with responsibility. It is not just a free ticket to an amusement park. It is not a ticket to escape the world around us or to evade the flames of hell. Your inheritance is a co-mission to co-labor with Christ to see his will be done on earth as it is in heaven. Creation is anxiously longing and waiting for you to claim your inheritance and become who you were meant to be. We live in a kingdom of the enfranchised, and what you have inherited, creation desperately needs. Salvation is not just to get you through the door of heaven, but it is to get heaven out into earth through you. As one who is seated with Christ Jesus in heavenly places, you are perfectly positioned to know God and make him known. Acting responsibly with our inheritance means that we embrace a life of co-laboring with Christ and take personal responsibility in the Kingdom of God.

Chapter 2

Called to Work

*"The heavens are the heavens of the Lord, But the earth he
has given to the sons of men."*(Psalm 115:16)

OUR INHERITANCE IN THE KINGDOM IS DEFINED by responsibility for
creation. During our lifetime, we are all responsible for managing a sphere
of influence in God's created order. The call to manage is the call to work.
This call is not to earn salvation but to co-labor with God to align creation with his original design. When we recognize the high calling of work
and the trust that God has extended to us within his creation, our labor
becomes supernatural in nature. All of creation is eagerly waiting for you
to embrace your calling and get to work! Once we are saved from sin
and death, we remain on earth because there is work to be done. We are
on the kingdom clock and now is the time to work. Christ is building his
kingdom, and he has called us to work alongside him in the family business.
Now, your identity qualifies you for your purpose. Christ's death and resurrection inaugurated the Kingdom of God, and you have been saved into
his present kingdom and the fullness to come. As a citizen of his kingdom,
we have inherited a privileged position and responsibility. God has called
us to co-labor with him in the family business. What exactly do we do in
this family business? Everything.

*"…in these last days has spoken to us in his Son, whom he appointed heir of all
things."*(Hebrews 1:2)

Everything and everyone in the Kingdom of God is important. There
are no insignificant or marginalized among those in God's house. Jesus
inherited everything, and so have you. The inheritance that Jesus received contained the keys to the kingdom — all authority. In Matthew

28:18b-19a, Jesus says, "…All authority has been given to Me in heaven and on earth. Go, therefore…"

When Jesus ascended after his resurrection, who did he leave in charge? Who received the Great Commission? The disciples. The word commission comes from the original Latin word *committere* which means "entrust." *Committere* is formed from two Latin words *com* which means "with" and *mittere* which means "send." Jesus has entrusted us as his disciples with a job description that sends us into a world that is unsettled by rebellion. The prince of the power of the air (Ephesians 2:2) must be subdued. Christ did not send us out unarmed. He sends us with the authority that he has been given — authority over all things in heaven and on earth.

In the authority of Christ, we must obey the commission "entrusted" to us. Like the original disciples, we are commissioned to go and do. There is nothing secular or mundane in day to day living. Everything is spiritual. Every action resonates in heaven and hell. Every motive and mindset shapes the world around us for better or worse. To the disciple, everyone and everything matters. Our lives are part of the answer to the Lord's Prayer, "Your kingdom come, your will be done, on earth as it is in heaven." (Matthew 6:10)

As co-heirs with Christ, we find it impossible to drift along through history caught in the currents of life and feeling that we have no purpose. Christians find it hard to have a passion for something that they believe they cannot affect. In truth, many of us feel that we cannot even steer the vessel of our lives much less make a difference in the kingdom. Over and over life seems to "happen to us" and we begin to feel that we may have never been intended to matter. Life seems to come and go in much the same way a small boat races down a quickly moving river without paddle or rudder. No matter what we believe intellectually or theologically about the nature of our boat, all of us spend our time trying to find our destination and steer our boat in that direction. We build, we love, we strive, we hope, we mourn, we fight, we believe, we work and we dream of something more. There is a deep and all-pervading script in the foundation of our being. This script was written by God and embedded in us from the time we were created. One can understand this core scripting, much like "hard coding" in a computer system.

The term "hard coding" (similar to the concept of hardwiring) in computer software refers the placement of specific programming values or framework that guides the software source code, and there is no way to override it. One of the hard-coded aspects of the human condition is that we all have a built-in periscope in our soul. This periscope is constantly seeking to find our maker and connect with eternity.

"He has made everything beautiful in its time. He has also set eternity in the human heart."(Ecclesiastes 3:11a)

The hard coding that God instilled in us quietly seeks to locate our maker and decode our purpose. It creates a desire to know the creator and manifests as a "God-shaped hole" in the soul.

Scripture indicates that Jesus is what people/nations desire even though they don't yet know him. Identified as the "desire of the nations," Haggai 2:7 says of him, "'And I will shake all nations, and they shall come to the desire of all nations, and I will fill this temple with glory,' says the Lord of hosts." (NKJV)

The attraction to the divine is part of our original design. We were designed to know God and to be conformed to the image of his likeness. Our entire being is hard-coded and constructed to seek out the divine and connect with our heavenly Father. We find that no matter where a person is from there is something in their design that desires God. As the scripture says, they all shall come to the Desire of All Nations. This desire draws us towards God, and when we find him, our identity is defined, and our design is complete.

Chapter 3
Designed to Shine

IN EPHESIANS, THE APOSTLE PAUL IS SPEAKING to the gentiles that are being saved and as they are being set apart from the cultural norms of sin that surround them. He loosely quotes Isaiah 60:1 over them as an exhortation. In this exhortation to lay hold of their identity in Christ and embrace the sanctification that leads to purpose, he says in Ephesians 5:14b-16, "'Awake, sleeper, And arise from the dead, And Christ will shine on you.' Therefore be careful how you walk, not as unwise men but as wise, making the most of your time, because the days are evil."

Deep down inside everyone knows they were designed for some special purpose. We were designed to shine.

"...you will shine among them like stars in the sky..."(Philippians 2:5)

Everyone has a deep need in their soul to matter, to know purpose, to be special. This awareness or desire to shine does not emanate from our fallen nature but our original design. It can become corrupted and manifest as pride and selfishness. However, this awareness of our inherent "specialness" comes from a deep awareness that we were made in the image of our Father. Our heavenly father is special, unique, beautiful, and of infinite worth. Something that shines by definition stands out against all that is around it. Your father shines and so do you.

"I, Jesus, have sent My angel to testify to you these things for the churches. I am the root and the descendant of David, the bright morning star."(Revelation 22:16)

Just as Jesus shines as the "bright and morning star," we also know deep in our being we are designed to shine. Jesus shines over and against all that is contrasted with him. You shine when you radiate the likeness of Jesus in the midst of the ashes and brokenness of the world around you. Just as Paul exhorted the believers in Ephesus so we must also be exhorted to Arise and Shine.

Knowing one's purpose is the rudder that guides our boat through the perils we experience all around us on this fast-moving river of life. Some would call it *destiny* or *calling*, but either way, purpose protects us from fate. Fate is where you end up without a rudder. Destiny is where you arrive by design. The original design was instilled or coded into our being to prod us onward in our search for purpose and meaning in life. Sadly, many who are in Christ have never realized that God originally designed them to be like the Father. We were designed to long for him and emulate him as we move through this short phase of eternity that we call life. Once we discover that purpose has been hard-coded into our very being, everything comes into focus. When the soul's God-shaped hole is filled with the presence of God through faith in Christ, our original design is realized, and our potential is activated.

Through understanding that God created you with an original design, meaning is restored to existence. A sense of eternal meaning will become evident, even in what may seem mundane. To find our destiny, we must reframe life into a kingdom context. Every follower of Christ must understand that their participation is vital in seeing his kingdom come and his will be done. Here is God's original design for mankind. As one who is born again you are called to participate with Christ in his grand kingdom enterprise.

I love this quote from the theologian N.T. Wright, regarding our purpose in the Kingdom of God.

> *"Salvation only does what it's meant to do when those who have been saved, are being saved, and will one day fully be saved realize that they are saved not as souls but as wholes and not for themselves alone but for what God now longs to do through them."*[2]

The Gospel of the Kingdom is all about the saving of whole human beings, not just the souls of men. The saving of one's soul is of the highest benefit to that individual, but when a person's entire life is holisti-

---

2 *N.T.Wright, Surprised By Hope, pg 199*

cally transformed the world around them also benefits. The kingdom is demonstrated when you shine according to your design. The dark places of this world are in desperate need of the sons of God to reflect the light of heaven into the worst corners of creation. Salvation is not just a means of escape from the misery in the world around us, but it is a commission to influence and align the world around you to heaven that is inside you.

N.T. Wright goes on to say:

"The point is this. When God saves people in this life, by working through his Spirit to bring them to faith in Jesus, in discipleship, prayer, holiness, hope, and love, such people are designed — it isn't too strong a word — to be a sign and foretaste of what God wants to do for the entire cosmos. What's more, such people are not just to be a sign and foretaste of that ultimate salvation; they are to be part of the means by which God makes this happen in both the present and the future."[3]

---

3 *Ibid. pg 199*

Chapter 4
Kingdom Context

*"The greatest issue facing the world today, with all its heartbreaking
needs, is whether those who, by profession or culture, are identified as
'Christians' will become disciples — students, apprentices, practitioners — of
Jesus Christ, steadily learning from him how to live the life of the Kingdom
of the Heavens into every corner of human existence."* (Dallas Willard)[4]

LACK OF CONTEXT IN LIFE LEADS TO insecurity and self-imposed marginalization. The key to finding purpose in life is to understand one's context. Regardless of our personal, political, or social inclinations, believers must realize that ultimately we are living in a kingdom. Eternal reality is a Monarchy ruled by the King of Kings and Lord of Lords. We are citizens of the kingdom of heaven first and citizens of geographic and political nations second. Quite far down the line of eternal relevance, we also have some form of ethnic origin that is a backdrop in our life.

If our context as believers is the Kingdom of God, it would be logical to explore the question "What is the kingdom?" Simply stated, the kingdom is the domain of the King. The domain of the King is where the King is ruling and reigning. He is reigning where he is recognized, and his authority is enforced. This is why Jesus said that the Kingdom of God is "within you." The kingdom is within every believer because one who is born again is submitted to God and constantly in the presence of the King. The believer is willingly under the authority of the King in an unbroken relationship of love and trust. By submitting to the King, you are under his authority, and you can, in turn, receive delegated authority to represent the King. This

---

4 *Dallas Willard, The Great Omission: Reclaiming Jesus' Essential Teachings on Discipleship.*

internal reality is why nothing in the world can separate you from God. No external force can alter your inner kingdom position unless you step out from under the authority of the King and submit to the wrong lord.

> *"God's kingdom is present in its beginnings, but still future in its fullness."* (Timothy J. Keller)

In any discussion about the Kingdom of God, there are many elements of mystery and valid room for discussion, but Jesus is clear when he says that the kingdom is near.

> *"The scribe said to him, 'Right, Teacher; you have truly stated that he is One, and there is no one else besides him; and to love him with all the heart and with all the understanding and with all the strength, and to love one's neighbor as himself, is much more than all burnt offerings and sacrifices.' When Jesus saw that he had answered intelligently, he said to him, 'You are not far from the Kingdom of God.'"* (Mark 12:32–34a)

Reassuringly, Jesus tells the scribe that responded intelligently about the ways of God that he was not far from the kingdom; in fact, he was standing next to the King.

As followers of Christ, we are called into service in his kingdom, much has been done, but much is yet to come. Jesus taught his disciples to pray, "Thy King come, thy will be done on earth as it is in heaven." We live in the most incredible season in spiritual history-the season of the kingdom "come" and kingdom "being done" on earth as it is in heaven.

Scripture clearly states that the Gospel was and is the Gospel of the King. Mark 1:14–15 says, "Jesus came into Galilee, preaching the gospel of God, and saying, 'The time is fulfilled, and the Kingdom of God is at hand; repent and believe in the gospel.'"

In Luke 17, Jesus proceeds to undermine Jewish assumptions about the coming Kingdom of God and to create enough mystery and controversy as to keep people intrigued. Today, we are still intrigued.

> *"Once, on being asked by the Pharisees when the Kingdom of God would come, Jesus replied, "The coming of the Kingdom of God is not something that can be observed, nor will people say, 'Here it is,' or 'There it is,' because the Kingdom of God is in your midst [within you]."* (Luke 17:20–21 NIV)

A primary concept that we should grasp from this passage is that the kingdom always functions from the internal to the external. It is first manifested on earth in the heart of those born again. From within the heart of the believer, the kingdom is released outward as influence empowered by authority. Jesus clearly says in this scripture that the Kingdom of God is not something that is imposed from outside in a political or in a natural sense. It is an internal reality that shapes the world around the Christ-follower. The means used to establish the kingdom are the true mystery that we will explore throughout the remainder of this study.

Luke records Jesus saying, "Nor will they say, 'Look, here it is!' or, 'Look, there it is.'" (Luke 17:21) The kingdom is within the believer because here the Lord has chosen to make his home. It is not geographically stationary or situated. It is not a building or structure, though it may very well affect those things. It is a tangible intangible just as Jesus is to everyone who believes.

The Kingdom of God is like a seed of life that is implanted in your heart when you believe and are regenerated. God's original design is that the seed of the Kingdom of God would grow and overflow from within your heart to influence the world around you. This process of growth first begins on the inside and then moves outward like the ripple effects of a stone thrown into a pond.

"First clean the inside of the cup and of the dish, so that the outside of it may become clean also." (Matthew 23:26b)

We see that Jesus is primarily concerned about the cleanliness or condition "inside of the cup" or the spiritual condition of a person's heart. Once the heart is cleansed and restored, the external condition will naturally begin to reflect the internal. The nature of the kingdom is to permeate outwards from a starting point that is connected to heaven. The Kingdom of God is not about behavior modification or external compliance to a set of rules. Outward pressure that attempts to produce inward change is a form of control. Control and compliance are not fruits of the spirit and are contrary to God's design.

The kingdom is all about voluntary internal transformation, not behavior modification. Behavior is important, but it is just a symptom, not the real issue. The real issue is that behaviors are just the manifestation of your internal beliefs and values. The guiding scriptural principle is that you become like the God (or gods) you serve. Problematic behavior is often due to a problematic belief system. How do we see true transformation and change in our lives and then in the world around us? Religion and politics say, "Submit, behave & comply," the Kingdom of God says, "Believe, behold & transform."

The kingdom is not a system of rules and regulations to be followed. It is the rule and reign of the King of Kings and Lord of Lords. The intriguing bit is that he implements his rule and reign over all of creation through his children — you and me. The Kingdom of God is a family business. You, as a child of God, truly do matter in the kingdom. Transformation happens through the transformed. Jesus transforms your heart though repentance and salvation, and in turn, you are given the charge to transform the world around you.

Chapter 5
Gardens and Kingdoms

"And he said, "How shall we picture the Kingdom of God, or by what parable shall we present it? It is like a mustard seed, which, when sown upon the soil, though it is smaller than all the seeds that are upon the soil, yet when it is sown, it grows up and becomes larger than all the garden plants and forms large branches; so that the birds of the air can nest under its shade." (Mark 4:30−32)

IN MARK 4, SCRIPTURE METAPHORICALLY REFERS TO the lesser spiritual kingdoms of this world as garden plants. The parable describes the manifested Kingdom of God as being the refuge and context for life, a place of nesting or a place called home. Ever since Jesus inaugurated the Kingdom of God on earth, the kingdom has been growing.

From the tiny seed of Jesus' life on earth, the kingdom is becoming the very presence of God filling all of creation. There are many other "garden plants" or "kingdoms," but the Kingdom of God will overtake and displace them all.

Scripture is filled with metaphoric and literal references to the rebellious lesser kingdoms or authority structures that the enemy has established in his ongoing rebellion against the one true God. These lesser kingdoms, or "authorities," are those that are associated with lowercase "g" gods in scripture. Before the cross, these lesser kingdoms (dominions) had strength and legitimacy due to Adam and Eve handing over their delegated authority through their sin. Everything changed when Jesus was unexpectedly resurrected. The enemy believed he had subdued the Christ through death on the cross and, therefore, was still in charge on earth. Suddenly he found himself "in subjection" under Christ's feet; creation was returned to the authority of the rightful King. The enemy had been outmaneuvered.

"I pray that the eyes of your heart may be enlightened, so that you will know what is the hope of his calling, what are the riches of the glory of his inheritance in the saints, and what is the surpassing greatness of his power toward us who believe. These are in accordance with the working of the strength of his might which he brought about in Christ, when he raised him from the dead and seated him at his right hand in the heavenly places, far above all rule and authority and power and dominion, and every name that is named, not only in this age but also in the one to come. And he put all things in subjection under his feet, and gave him as head over all things to the church, which is his body, the fullness of him who fills all in all." (Ephesians 1:18–23)

The principalities and powers (verse 21) that the apostle Paul refers to in the book of Ephesians are often referred to as lower case "g" gods, particularly in the Old Testament. These gods and their lesser kingdoms, or authority structures in creation, are also referred to as "hills" and "mountains." Once we take into account the metaphoric meaning of these terms, many passages take on a whole new supernatural depth. One example is repeated in both Isaiah 2:2 and Micah 4:1.

"Now it will come about that in the last days, the mountain of the house of the Lord will be established as the chief of the mountains, and will be raised above the hills; and all the nations will stream to it." (Isaiah 2:2)

The mountain of the house of the Lord is referring to the Kingdom of God. God's kingdom is prophesied to be raised above or in authority over the "hills." The "hills" are the lesser kingdoms or authority structures set up by the little "g" gods, or principalities and powers. It is evident from this scripture that what has kept the nations from coming to the Lord are these little "g" gods. The hills were set against the knowledge of God throughout history and are still seen to resist the work of the Gospel even when the Kingdom of Heaven has come upon them. Satan's strategy seems to be to cover up the epic defeat he suffered at the cross and keep people under his control through not allowing them to see the light.

The apostle Paul returns to this understanding of the work of Satan that prevents people from receiving the Gospel. He says in 2 Corinthians 4:4, "in whose case the god of this world has blinded the minds of the unbelieving so that they might not see the light of the gospel of the glory of Christ, who is the image of God."

Now that the Kingdom of God is established, the nations stream to the mountain or "authority" structure of God. They are flooding in through the narrow gate of salvation. If you live in the same reality that I do you also are very aware of the continued opposition and subversion instigated by the "hills" and those that submit to them through worship. Wars, poverty, hopelessness, hunger, perversion, and pride still emanate through those that bow down to these gods. Though Jesus took back all authority from the enemy and his kingdom of little hills at the cross, there are plenty of people who choose the kingdom of darkness over the kingdom of light. Through ignorance and sin, they submit to the lesser hills and prop up these failed spiritual states. Jesus moved decisively and violently against the lesser spiritual kingdoms through his death and resurrection. The book of Colossians describes their defeat and subjugation.

"And having disarmed the powers and authorities, he made a public spectacle of them, triumphing over them by the cross."(Colossians 2:15)

This scripture shows that when Jesus disarmed the hills (powers), these lesser "powers and authorities" where shockingly subjected to the mountain of the house of the Lord. He has become Chief over the hills. The spiritual order was completely restored to its original design.

Chapter 6
Spiritual Sea Change

THE PROPHET ISAIAH DESCRIBED THE EXPANSION OF the kingdom saying, "...for the earth will be filled with the knowledge of the Lord as the waters cover the sea." (Isaiah 11:9b NIV)

We are living in the middle of the greatest transformational sea change in spiritual history, and we have the privilege to be commissioned as co-heirs with Christ. No matter who we are, where we are, or what we are called to do, as believers, we are on mission. We are on a cooperative mission or co-mission with Jesus to undermine the works of the devil and destroy the fiefdoms of the little plants in the garden.

> *"And he said, "How shall we picture the Kingdom of God, or by what parable shall we present it? It is like a mustard seed, which, when sown upon the soil, though it is smaller than all the seeds that are upon the soil, yet when it is sown, it grows up and becomes larger than all the garden plants and forms large branches; so that the birds of the air can nest under its shade." (Mark 4:30–32)*

Here scripture mentions "other seeds that are upon the ground." These "other seeds" end up being out-shined by the tiny mustard seed that grows up to extend over everything else in the garden. The counterfeit or lesser seeds produce an inferior kingdom. With their authority contained and overshadowed by the Kingdom of God. The seeds of the enemy are as potted plants that think they are the source of life and equally as viable as God. Each of these desires to be *the* garden plant and attain the worship of mankind. They long to be seen as God, worshiped as God, and function as God. But the Kingdom of God is greater. Greater than all.

Then comes the little mustard seed that overcomes and overshadows everything else in the cosmos. This little seed seemed so nonthreatening when it was born in a barn to an average Jewish craftsman. This unimpressive seed turned out to be the tree of life. Now that the seed is planted and growing it has become "larger than all the garden plants." Creation has again regained access to its true source of life, Jesus Christ. What was lost through Adam's sin in the Garden of Eden has been restored through the sinless sacrifice of the second Adam.

> *"Pray, then, in this way: 'Our Father who is in heaven, Hallowed be your name. Your kingdom come. Your will be done, On earth as it is in heaven. Give us this day our daily bread. And forgive us our debts, as we also have forgiven our debtors. And do not lead us into temptation, but deliver us from evil. For yours is the kingdom and the power and the glory forever. Amen.'"* (Matthew 6:9–13)

The seed is planted, and the greatest of the "garden plants" (the Kingdom of God) is growing and expanding. The Lord's Prayer contains all the perfect purposes of God the Father and calls out all the God-given potential of his children. You have been given the ultimate privilege and responsibility to work alongside your heavenly father to see answers to this prayer. There are no second class Christians in the kingdom. All who follow Christ are equally called and commissioned to participate with God to see his kingdom come, and his will be done on earth as it is in heaven.

> *"You are from God, little children, and have overcome them; because greater is he who is in you than he who is in the world."* (1 John 4:4)

You were designed and empowered to define the world around you. You were designed to overcome and not be overcome. You are from God, and you are part of his kingdom that cannot be shaken. *You have the light of Christ burning in your redeemed soul.*

> *"Therefore since we receive a kingdom which cannot be shaken, let us show gratitude, by which we may offer to God an acceptable service with reverence and awe;"* (Hebrews 12:28)

We are born again as followers of Christ into an epic storm that rages all around. This storm is the aftermath of Jesus' victory at the cross, the greatest battle of all time. The Kingdom of God arrived through the decisive action taken at the cross to reclaim all authority in heaven and earth. When Jesus was raised from the dead, he defeated the devil and took back the keys to life and death. What Adam gave away Jesus reclaimed.

The Bible says that where the first Adam had failed through sin, the second Adam (Christ) overcame sin and death and took his place at the right hand of God. His kingdom has come, is coming and will come. Jesus announced his authority and re-commissioned his followers in Matthew 28:18–19b, "And Jesus came up and spoke to them, saying, "All authority has been given to Me in heaven and on earth. Go, therefore…""

We now find ourselves empowered with delegated authority from the King of Kings and Lord of Lords. Our mandate is clear, and as we step out to "go" in obedience to the design of God, we find ourselves walking securely during any storm. We have received a kingdom that cannot be shaken and our feet stand on steady ground. Our identity, context, and purpose are secure.

Chapter 7
The Great Dissipation

"Where there is no revelation, people cast off restraint; but blessed is the one who heeds wisdom's instruction." (Proverbs 29:18 NIV)

COMFORT IS OFTEN THE ENEMY OF VISION and complacency the enemy of our purpose. The challenge of our era is that we have not developed a "vision" for the Kingdom of God. Due to our lack of vision, we find little reason to "restrain" or "constrain" our choices. I believe this proverb says that if we do not want to perish in body, soul, and spirit, we must choose to limit our options. We must define our life context and choose to "restrain" our capacity. We live in a world of ever-increasing options. Unlimited entertainment and access to a myriad of activities at any given moment make it all the more important that we seek to focus in our lives. The challenge of our day is to avoid the sin of dissipation. Dissipation can be envisioned like smoke that starts out as a hot, dense fire and then disappears as it drifts away, becoming nothing. This is the essence of living without purpose, and it is a visual of the life lived without understanding. The apostle Peter draws a clear distinction between how a believer is supposed to live, versus the dissipated life. He said:

"In regard to these, they think it strange that you do not run with them in the same flood of dissipation, speaking evil of you." (1 Peter 4:4 NKJV)

When you choose to live with "restraint," then you are blessed by wisdom, according to Proverbs 29:18. Dissipation is the only alternative to life in the kingdom. You either focus or you fade.

You have to choose. What will empower a person to choose one thing above another is if the "one thing" seems to be the most valuable. We must have a compelling vision which empowers us to constrain or "focus" our

choices to reach our potential. God has created you in his image and likeness. You are built and hard-coded or "wired" to desire a relationship with
God and to radiate hope and purpose. You fit perfectly into the kingdom,
and the kingdom fits perfectly in you. This is how you were designed. Purpose creates confidence that gives us hope. Our purpose is realized through
reaching out to the life of heaven, the presence of God, while grasping the
hand of those who live in shadow. This is to co-labor with God.

In our era in spiritual history, the body of Christ is rightfully beginning
to ask the question, "Now what?" Part of the answer lies in gaining an understanding of what came first. What was clear from the beginning should
inform what seems now to be dimly visible. The apostle Paul expresses
his struggle with the reality that things are often unclear, even to one as
faithful to God as Paul was.

> "For now we see in a mirror dimly, but then face to face; now I know in part, but
> then I will know fully just as I also have been fully known." (1st Corinthians
> 13:12)

Looking back to the original design, or the original picture that is painted by God in Genesis, we can shed more light on what seems dim and gain
an actionable understanding of our purpose.

There is some scripture that seems hard to understand and is open
to various interpretations. Often scripture seems to be only seen "dimly." Even the Apostle Peter, when referencing Paul's writings in 2 Peter
3:15—16, indicates that some of what Paul writes is hard to understand.
Peter said, "... and regard the patience of our Lord as salvation; just as also
our beloved brother Paul, according to the wisdom given him, wrote to
you, as also in all his letters, speaking in them of these things, in which are
some things hard to understand..."

Regardless of the parts of scripture that are difficult to understand, I
suggest that a transformational kingdom narrative is readily visible when
the entirety of scripture is considered. This narrative can easily be grasped
by any believer and serves to rebuild the foundation of purpose from
which we often drift.

Though much is seen only "dimly" as Paul says, this narrative of hope
and purpose we are exploring will stand out vividly once the painting is
complete. Each element in this study aims to illustrate our position and
purpose in the kingdom. To move forward, we have to look back; other-

wise, we have no way to measure our journey. Let's go back to God's original design for creation and explore the original commission he bestowed on those that bare his image and likeness, mankind.

We find in scripture an overwhelmingly and compelling story or "Meta-Narrative." A Meta-Narrative is a Grand Story or a "story arc" that encompasses the past, present, and future like a rainbow. Understanding your position in this story arc, positions you to realize meaning in life. Where do you fit in the story arc? What is your purpose? All believers are given a shining moment in the story arc of eternity.

Acting on the understanding that you are designed with purpose is the only antidote to the cultural drift that kills the soul and pulls creation away from the kingdom. Even within Christian circles, this drift into dissipation is commonplace. Amid dissipation, we look for entertainment to give us hope and social opinion to provide our purpose. We grasp at these temporary illusions because we lack the revelation of God's original design. Only his design gives us purpose and brings the world hope. Unless we find our identity and calling in the kingdom, we become content to abdicate responsibility for the condition of the world around us. Once we abdicate, we "run with them into the flood of dissipation." Suddenly we realize that our purpose and potential is vanishing like a brief morning mist.

The writer in Proverbs 29:18 wisely observes that without vision, the human condition declines and perishes. What many have lost or possibly never even realized, is the vision set forward by God from the beginning of time. A vision for the kingdom gives us our shining moment of purpose and gives creation a hope and a future.

Chapter 8
The Original Design

"In the beginning God created the heavens and the earth." (Genesis 1:1)

ONE HELPFUL WAY TO LOOK AT CREATION is as computer hardware. God created the perfect platform or "hardware" and called it "good." Genesis 1:31a says, "God saw all that he had made, and behold, it was very good…" We find our heavenly Father created a perfectly designed environment for his children. Adam and Eve were placed as his first children into his garden, his earth, his universe.

A simple illustration that can help us understand the created order is to think of it as an infinitely advanced computer system or "hardware" that was built to run on the software of heaven. The software of heaven, combined with the hardware of creation, created a perfect "operating system." God's software and his hardware are perfectly compatible. By design, this operating system co-mingled heaven and earth. The first working example of multidimensional human existence was modeled in the Garden of Eden. It was God's original design that mankind would be both spiritual and natural in their created nature.

"He is before all things, and in him, all things hold together." (Colossians 1:17)

Through his matchless wisdom and knowledge, God wrote the perfect software that "holds all things together." His power and software, combined with his hardware, created the perfect operating system.

"I will give thanks to you, for I am fearfully and wonderfully made; Wonderful are your works, And my soul knows it very well." (Psalm 139:14)

The Garden of Eden was a perfect environment into which God introduced mankind into his created order. Once created, mankind was placed into a context that was a perfect example of what all of creation was intended to become. God designed creation to require the work of mankind for it to fulfill its design. His original design required a co-laboring relationship with mankind to operate the system that he had created.

Before the fall of man when sin corrupted creation, God's perfect operating system was on full display. A beautiful system designed by God, who as the author of all things, retains the right to define beauty and order. He reveals beauty and order by revealing his nature and likeness as expressed through creation. Like our creator, the story of creation is beautiful. It is a story of beauty wrapped in awe-inspiring moments that teach us to fear God and draw us to love our creator. When we are honest, our soul reminds us that we live in a universe that was designed with precision and beauty. This revelation inspires wonder and fear and compels us to connect with our creator.

We fear God in the sense that we recognize his awesome power to create worlds with his words. Marvelous wonders such as human beings made by his hands. We also fear God in that we know that we exist at his pleasure. We know that he is infinite and we are not. We also fear God in that we are reverently grateful. The one who rightly fears God recognizes that he designed a place for us in his kingdom and that the Lord knows our name.

Scripture says that he knows how many hairs are on your head. Our deepest desire is to be known and loved, and God desires that he would be known and loved by us. This is truly a match made in heaven. Our souls also long to know where we came from, where we are going, and why. The desire for identity is hard-wired into our very being and drives much of our behavior. This desire to be known and valued is part of God's perfect operating system. Deep inside, we know that we are inherently valuable and that we were designed to matter.

Mankind bears God's "image and likeness," and each person carries a reflection of the heavenly father. Part of being created in the image and likeness of God means that we carry aspects of his nature by design. It is in God's nature to create, to build and to relate and so we as his children carry these same desires. We sense eternity in our hearts and those that have eternity in mind realize they are designed to shine.

Chapter 9
Theology of Work

"SETTING THE STAGE" IS A COMMONLY USED idiom in the English language. The expression comes from the terminology used in theatre to describe setting up the various elements on the stage of a play or theatre production. Another definition of this expression is "preparing the way for something else to happen." Setting the stage is essentially creating the context.

Understanding the context in which God placed Adam and Eve is extremely helpful to understand our original design in a better fashion. Why did God set the stage the way he did at the beginning? Context gives us perspective, and proper perspective informs understanding. Once our understanding is truthfully informed we can much more readily discern our purpose in God's original design. To best build out a practical theology for work (vocation), mission and meaning, let's start at the beginning. The divine origins of work can be discovered by exploring where work was first established.

"The Lord God planted a garden toward the east, in Eden; and there he placed the man whom he had formed." (Genesis 2:8)

The story of creation opens with not only the explosion of life on earth and in the cosmos but also the creation of God's pinnacle of self-expression, mankind.

"God created man in his own image, in the image of God he created him; male and female he created them." (Genesis 1:27)

Adam and Eve were placed in a garden, in the east of Eden. Most believers are familiar with this location, commonly known as the Garden of Eden.

There is vital imagery that we see right from the beginning. There are three distinct geographical areas referred to in the creation narrative. Imagine that you are looking at the earth from space at the time of the creation. You would see the earth as a whole, and Eden an area of exceptional life and beauty, and if you zoomed way in you would see a certain small piece of paradise. You would see the Garden of Eden. A defining feature of the garden was that a river that flowed into it from Eden. From the garden, this river split into four rivers and flowed out into the rest of the earth.

"Now a river flowed out of Eden to water the garden; and from there it divided and became four rivers." (Genesis 2:10)

We keep in mind this reference to a river flowing in from Eden and out from the garden as we build our theology of work. The mention of the river entering the garden and the four rivers flowing outward carry significant meaning in the scriptural meta-narrative we are exploring. The imagery of the rivers that flow with life-giving water become a key point of reference and imagery for those who are redeemed and live under the new covenant.

As we have seen, there are three distinct regions mentioned in the Genesis account of creation. These geographical elements, established at creation, symbolically set the stage for God's kingdom on earth. Surprisingly, these geographic arrangements are significant to understanding our identity as followers of Christ. The way the stage is set at the very beginning of a production helps give context to the story. You and I are still somewhere in the middle of this intricate, yet redemptive narrative that God is weaving together as his kingdom unfolds. Together with his children, God is writing this story. He has chosen in his sovereignty to let you have a meaningful co-authoring role in his meta-narrative of creation. Our cumulative experience as mankind exists in a story of love, heartbreak, transformation, and restoration.

Co-Laboring

"Then the Lord God formed man of dust from the ground, and breathed into his nostrils the breath of life; and man became a living being." (Genesis 2:7)

In Genesis 2, we revisit a specific "day" in the midst of the overall
creation story that was generally covered in Genesis 1. The specific day in
question is the day that God created mankind with his own hands from the
dust of the earth and breathed his spirit into the first man. Spiritual reality
was imparted to what he created. Mankind was created as spirit and flesh.

"Then God said, "Let Us make man in Our image, according to Our likeness;"
(Genesis 1:26a)

According to Genesis, all elements of God's creation were spoken into
being, except for mankind. God carefully shaped Adam from the dust of
the earth and breathed life into this work of his hands and then Eve was
shaped from the extracted rib of Adam through which she also bore the
image and likeness of God. From the beginning, mankind was a multi-dimensional being. They were spirit and flesh. They were designed to relate
to heaven and to host the presence of God on earth. A unique aspect of
Adam and Eve's role in creation was that they were designed to manage
their vertical relationship with God and manage their horizontal relationship with the rest of creation. What they received by direct relationship
with God enabled them to influence, horizontally, all of creation. Their
top-line responsibility was to their relationship with their father, for whom
they were created.

Just before this specific description of the creation of Adam and Eve, we
see a significant comment. The scripture indicates that the rest of creation
was waiting for mankind to arrive on the scene.

*"Now no shrub of the field was yet in the earth, and no plant of the field had yet
sprouted, for the Lord God had not sent rain upon the earth, and there was no
man to cultivate the ground."* (Genesis 2:5)

Verse five indicates that what God had created was full of potential that
had not been fully released. The process of growth, life, and fullness were
in a holding pattern until mankind arrived. The operating system of creation was designed to require the meaningful involvement of mankind. The
earth was waiting for mankind to take up their commission to work. The
fruitfulness and potential of God's creation were designed to be awakened
when mankind worked. Creation was designed to require mankind to
fulfill a co-laboring role with God. Mankind would work, and God would
send the rain, then the earth would bloom. Genesis 2:5 indicates that

mankind was purpose-built to cultivate creation and see its full potential brought to life.

The Original Commission

"God blessed them; and God said to them, 'Be fruitful and multiply, and fill the earth, and subdue it; and rule over the fish of the sea and over the birds of the sky and over every living thing that moves on the earth.'" (Genesis 1:28)

This statement sets into motion what is known as the Original Commission. This mandate came to Adam and Eve and set the original design of God into motion for the rest spiritual history. At this moment, they received the commission that would provide purpose and meaning to the rest of mankind. The delegation of responsibility for the rest of creation and the impartation of authority would legitimize their right to rule. God made creation to require their administration. They had to *work* for creation to *work*. At this moment work was given dignity and connected mankind with the divine.

As soon as Adam and Eve receive the breath of life, they find themselves gainfully employed. God immediately orients them to the original design of creation. They are commissioned to release all the potential in creation. God left a lot of work to be done. He expressly intended to co-labor with his children to see creation reach its full potential. Creation rises into its purpose when Mankind takes up their calling to cultivate. The original commission is the primary stone set in the foundation of the theology of work. As such it is of great importance that we take a close look at the meaning of the word *commission*. The English word *commission* has several varying definitions based on its particular use as a noun, verb, etc. To understand what Adam and Eve were receiving from God, let's look at two specifically relevant definitions of the word commission.

1. *a group of people who have been formally chosen and given the authority to get information about a problem or to perform other special duties.*
2. *to formally choose someone to do a special piece of work, or to formally ask for a special piece of work from someone.*
   (The Cambridge Dictionary)

From these definitions, we see that it incorporates several elements.

1. A formal choosing for a role — Identity
2. Authorization to carry out a role — Authority
3. Perform or to carry out a role — Ability

Commissioned to Work!

What was Adam's original commission? Taking responsibility to see the world outside of the garden become like the world inside the garden. To accomplish this original commission, the Lord gave him the following resources:

1. the model (the Garden of Eden)
2. the delegated authority (the commission)
3. the method (be fruitful and multiply, expand and fill the earth)
4. the means (cultivate it and keep it — work).

We see God outline mankind's purpose by giving them an epic job description and a commission to refine creation. God gave to Adam and Eve identity, delegated authority and the ability to fulfill their commission to rule over creation. What God gave them he also gives you. You have the same original commission, and you have what it takes to fulfill the same high calling. Now life gets really meaningful. We get to work alongside our heavenly Father to see his will be done on earth as it is in heaven. To embrace our commission, we need to embrace the means through which the kingdom is established. You are called to work! You are a vital lifeline between heaven and earth.

"Individually the disciple and friend of Jesus who has learned to work shoulder to shoulder with his or her Lord stands in this world as a point of contact between heaven and earth, a kind of Jacob's ladder by which the angels of God may ascend from and descend into human life. Thus the disciple stands as an envoy or a receiver by which the Kingdom of God is conveyed into every quarter of human affairs." (Dallas Willard)[5]

---

5 *Dallas Willard, Hearing God: Developing a Conversational Relationship with God*

Managing your metron is all about being the disciple that conveys the Kingdom of God into every dark and desperate corner of human affairs.

You are not only permitted to work; you are commissioned to work. You have received delegated authority from God to fulfill the same role given to Adam and Eve. The original commission is as much for you today as it was for Adam and Eve in the garden. In fact, you too have a garden within which your call to work is established.

What is my garden you might ask? Your garden is any *sphere of influence* in which God has placed you and where you manage relationship vertically with God and laterally into creation. This sphere of influence can metaphorically be described as your "garden of Eden." Within your garden you are commissioned to rule. The way you rule is the same way that Adam and Eve were called to rule. When you reach out and touch heaven while your feet stand on earth, it is like you are laying hold of a high voltage power line and serving as a conduit through which the presence of God lights up your sphere of influence.

To properly understand how vital your calling to work is, you must see it as the lifeline between heaven and earth. Your work enables the latent seeds of potential to come to life all around you. Understanding the fundamental nature of work as vocation, you can not help but wake up each day excited to set your feet on the job floor. The highlight of your day is when you reach up to lay hold of heaven. Your vocation is the primary means through which the kingdom comes, and his will is done on earth as it is in heaven. As a follower of Christ, you have been given the model, authority, and means to change the world one workday at a time. Too many of us have a sin tainted, low view of work. We need to revisit the concept of vocation and discover God's original design. Creation is waiting on you!

> "Then the Lord God took the man and put him into the garden of Eden to cultivate it and keep it." (Genesis 2:15)

The theology of work can be summed up as "Work is Good — Work was before the Fall and is not a result of the Fall." The original commission was given to mankind before the fall. The timing of God's command to Adam and Eve is important to note as it places work in its proper context. God declared that all of his creation was good, and the concept of work was part of God's creation. Work was part of the original design, and it too was declared "good." In the original commission, we see that work was established *before* sin or the fall, not a *result* of sin or the fall.

A common misconception is that work was a result of sin and is some form of punishment from God that came upon all mankind because of Adam. The truth is that work is good because it came from God, and it is part of God's nature to work. To align with God's design and to work is a direct act of obedience. All obedience is an act of worship. Work is fundamentally a form of worship. Thus we discover that work is spiritual, like all forms of worship are spiritual. Mankind was hard-wired by God with a desire to work. You were given permission and a commission to work. By working you are walking in obedience, and that obedience is noticed by the Lord.

There is nothing wrong with embracing your God-given compulsion to create, build, develop, prosper, and accomplish through work. When labor is done as unto the Lord it becomes worship that reaches the throne room of God. Work makes a difference to God and creation is waiting on you to co-labor with your Father to release its potential. For creation to thrive, it needs something from God and something from mankind.

Creation is waiting on you

"Now no shrub of the field was yet in the earth, and no plant of the field had yet sprouted, for the Lord God had not sent rain upon the earth, and there was no man to cultivate [work or serve] the ground." (Genesis 2:5)

Creation was designed to require mankind to take responsibility to work and to steward it. There is abundance ready to bloom, but God holds back the latent potential found in creation until his people are ready to co-labor. When mankind doesn't cultivate or "work," then human purpose is lost, and creation suffers. Looking back at Genesis 2:5 we see how creation was waiting on mankind to be in a position to cultivate it before the potential that was contained in its seeds would come to life — living according to God's original design matters. It matters to us personally, and it matters even to the physical and spiritual condition of the world around us.

Work is sacred and not a curse. Work is the intended means by which all of mankind is to cooperate with God to subdue creation. The original design established mankind as the delegated authority who was charged with stewarding creation.

Work is a high calling!

"To explore the truth of God's call is to appreciate what is nothing less than God's grand global project for the restoration and renewal of humanity and the earth — and our part in it."(Os Guinness)[6]

When work is recognized as a calling, then dignity is restored to vocation. If the spiritual design of vocation is not recognized then labor will always be viewed as a curse and something to be avoided.

Every human attracted to productive activity, or work, according to their original design. Our work is given to us by God just as Adam and Eve received their assignment from the Lord. God gives us a *calling* to work.

The term *calling* is defined as "a strong inner impulse toward a particular course of action, especially when accompanied by conviction of divine influence: the vocation or profession in which one customarily engages." [7]

Adam and Eve were given a calling from the beginning. Since the first call to work in the Garden of Eden, mankind has been driven by a hardwired desire to improve upon creation. Deep within all humans, regardless of culture or background, there is a compelling pull in their soul to build, improve, provide and steward. This impulse is not abnormal. It is a direct alignment with the character and image of the creator God. By some means we all know that our identity and purpose is expressed through our work. This compulsion can become idolatry if it is tainted by sin, but that doesn't mean that the instinct to work is wrong. It is very right, and you are very much called to work. When one obeys their calling, that calling becomes their vocation. Your vocation matters to creation and is given to you by the creator himself.

---

6 *Os Guinness, The Call, page xi*
7 *merriam-webster.com*

What does the word *vocation* actually mean? The Merriam Webster dictionary states that vocation is "a summons or strong inclination to a particular state or course of action."

When vocation is understood as a calling, we can answer difficult questions in life such as:

- Why do I sense a lack of purpose in my life?
- Why do I feel trapped in what may be considered the "ordinary?"
- I feel compelled to do something "extraordinary," but why do I feel I'm being punished by having to work a day job?
- Why do I feel trapped by responsibilities?
- Why do some people get to do spiritual work and I have to do secular work?

These are legitimate feelings that all Christians wrestle with during the course of life. Through a changing of the mind or worldview, we can find purpose and deep meaning in the work that fills our day to day existence. When you find *calling* in your *vocation*, then what seems to be *ordinary* becomes *extraordinary*!

"And I heard a voice from heaven, saying, 'Write, "Blessed are the dead who die in the Lord from now on!"' 'Yes,' says the Spirit, 'so that they may rest from their labors, for their deeds follow with them.'"(Revelation 14:13)

What could be more extraordinary than knowing that what you do day to day can actually follow you into eternity? Would we treat the work of our hands differently if we realized that we were not leaving it all behind when we die? What if your response to the Original Commission was intended to help shape eternity? It would be in keeping with God's original design to involve his children as co-laborers both in this life and in the resurrected life to come.

One day, we will rule and reign with the Lord and even sit in judgment over the activities of angels (1 Corinthians 6:3). You can look forward to a very active and meaningful role in God's eternity. This eternal work starts now and flows into God's heavenly order. Scripture indicates that the very work or labor that you rest from when you die will follow you as "deeds." If you "die in the Lord" you are blessed, and your work follows you into eternity. Scripture does not give an exact description of what one's works look like or how they translate into eternity, but the effects of your deeds are obvious to the world around you. The ripple effects of your actions are empowered by the authority that God delegated to you in the original commission. You are co-laboring with God right through into eternity.

The word "labors" in Revelation 14:13 is also translated as "work" and is translated from the Greek word *ergon*. *Ergon* is defined as the tangible work of your hands.

In his writing on the nature and purpose of work, theologian Anthony Hoekema puts forward a compelling thought when he writes, "One could also say that whatever people have done on this earth which glorified God will be remembered in the life to come: Revelation 14:13. But more must be said. Is it too much to say that, according to these verses, the unique contribution of each nation to the life of the present earth will enrich the life of the New Earth? Shall we then perhaps inherit the best products of culture and art which the earth has produced?"

Referring back to Revelations 14:13 he goes on to say, "Here we see the works for which man was created (Gen 2:15) and later redeemed (Ephesians 2:10) apparently being taken into eternity!"[8]

I find that the value we place on work or vocation is directly connected to the perspective we have about eternity. If we do not believe that the work matters in eternity, then we default to a low view of work. It becomes a nuisance and something to be avoided even if we spiritualize our low view of work by referring to it as legitimate spiritual activity. I have even heard Christian professionals warn others not to let work get in the way of what is spiritually important. This just serves to illustrate the confusion and deception that have conspired to denigrate the original commission and potentially limit your reward in heaven.

Indicators that you have a low view of work include:

1. You do not embrace the original commission
2. You do not believe that work is spiritual and natural
3. You do not believe that work matters to eternity
4. You abdicate responsibility for creation
5. You consciously or subconsciously believe that work is a result of sin
6. You believe that labor is itself a curse

---

8 *Anthony Hoekema (1913–1988), The Bible and the Future*

"For we are his workmanship, created in Christ Jesus for good works, which God prepared beforehand so that we would walk in them." (Ephesians 2:10)

Embracing a high view of vocation is in alignment with God's original design. Living in line with God's original design means we are not just saved *from* something, but you are also saved *to* something! Recognizing that you are called to something gets right to the heart of purpose.

Calling is rooted in purpose, purpose is rooted in your identity, and your identity is given by God. You are chosen or called. God declares your identity as the chosen. Scripture says, "But you are a chosen people, a royal priesthood, a holy nation, God's special possession, that you may declare the praises of him who called you out of darkness into his wonderful light." (1 Peter 2:9)

You are positioned and commissioned to work. You are positioned as a lifeline between heaven and earth, and your connection to heaven allows your sphere of influence to breathe its atmosphere. When you connect with your identity as a member of God's family you find that you are saved from sin and death and yet you are also saved to something. You are saved to the work of the kingdom. When a high view of work is embraced your vocation becomes a joy-filled, kingdom-building activity in which we co-labor with our father, God.

Indicators that you have a high view of work include:

1. You value work at the same level God values work
2. You recognize work as eternal in value
3. You embrace work as a form of worship
4. You embrace the original commission as God's design
5. You take responsibility for creation
6. You believe that work is an expression of the character and nature of God

A high view of work requires us to value work in the same manner God does. As followers of Christ, we are to align our value system with his value system. God honors work, and we too should honor what he values. Every follower of Christ is called to work. Your vocation is a sacred calling, and your labor is of eternal significance in the Kingdom of God. This is true regardless of the daily job held or the responsibilities you bear. The high view of work is there at the very beginning of God's word. How does this original commission define our lives as new covenant believers?

"In the beginning God created the heavens and the earth." (Genesis 1:1)

God created all that exists and that he had an original design in mind from the beginning of time. Genesis 1:28 goes on to say, "God blessed them; and God said to them..." The big idea of this verse is that when God commands us to do something, he also gives us the means to obey.

In Scripture, we see that the means God gave mankind was "authority." Delegated authority is the foundation of the Original Commission. We have delegated authority and were given the ability to serve as his agents. God put mankind in charge of creation and gave us a job description via Adam and Eve. Genesis 1:28 explains the Original Commission when it says, "God blessed them; and God said to them, 'Be fruitful and multiply, and fill the earth, and subdue it; and rule over the fish of the sea and over the birds of the sky and over every living thing that moves on the earth.'"

Let's look deeper into this scripture and extract the key elements that create the Original Commission.

*"God **blessed** them;"* (God gave them the means through imparted authority)

*"and God **said** to them,"* (God gave them a command)

*"**Be** fruitful and multiply, and fill the earth, and subdue it;"* (God anointed or empowered them)

*"and **rule over** the fish of the sea and over the birds of the sky and over every living thing that moves on the earth."* (God gave them a job description)

This original commission might seem far removed from us as believers, and you may be asking yourself, does this original design still apply to me? If so, how? The answer is yes and through co-laboring. God never withdrew his original commission to mankind. He continued to reinforce it and recommission his servants to align their lives with his vision for creation. He does not leave man alone to do this great work, and he is never far from those who take his commands seriously and seek to obey. Your obedience to any command of the Lord attracts the presence and favor of God. He draws close to those who draw close to him, and he works closely with those who work with him.

God's original commission was that mankind would co-labor with him to rule over the creation. No matter what we do in life, this mandate still applies. It is the nature and character of God to involve you in his business. He wants you to co-labor with him in the family business of the kingdom.

Co-Laboring by Design

"For every house is built by someone, but the builder of all things is God." (Hebrews 3:4)

Scripture reveals God as the master creator. He is the original artist and builder. Any aware individual who pauses to consider the creation around him will be quickly overwhelmed by the beauty and mesmerizing design. All creativity originates from the character and nature of God. He is more than capable of having finalized all aspects of creation in every respect, but as seen in scripture, he had something else in mind. Scripture says that God has prepared a pathway of good acts or works that the saved are called to walk.

"For we are his workmanship, created in Christ Jesus for good works, which God prepared beforehand so that we would walk in them." (Ephesians 2:10)

God's ultimate design was for an intimate, personal relationship with his children. This is why God does not just accomplish all labor himself. He chose to co-labor with mankind as an expression of intimacy and trust. This aspect of God's original design continues to be evident throughout scripture and is highlighted again by the apostle Paul when he speaks to the purpose of transformed believers.

God chose mankind to oversee and develop what he had created. Even as he placed Adam and Eve into the position of delegated authority over creation. He intentionally left many things unfinished. God made room for mankind to matter. You have to work for creation to work. This is also a function of God's original design. The participation and input of his children was a required element of his created order. Father God still makes room for his kids. Scripture explains several things God left unfinished by design.

1. **Multiply:** In Genesis 1:28, God commands Adam to "be fruitful and

multiply." So we find that God immediately gives Adam and Eve the responsibility for reproducing and populating the earth. God could have created billions of people all at the same time to fill the earth, but he chose to have Adam and Eve take responsibility for the purposes of God in this regard.

2. **Subdue:** Also, in Genesis 1:28, Adam and Eve are commanded to "subdue and rule" the earth. The obvious takeaway from this command is that the "earth" in its original created form, was not yet under authority or subjugation. The King of Heaven could have easily created a preformatted "earth" that was entirely like the garden, but he chose to have Adam and Eve take the responsibility to conform the condition of "earth" (that which was outside the garden) into the condition that was seen inside the garden.

3. **Name:** A clear illustration of God's desire to co-labor with his children was when he brought all the animals before Adam to be named. "Out of the ground the LORD God formed every beast of the field and every bird of the sky, and brought them to the man to see what he would call them; and whatever the man called a living creature, that was its name." (Genesis 2:19)

These few examples from Genesis illustrate that God *intentionally* left things unfinished. It is his will for you to co-author creation. In fact, mankind has constantly co-labored with God, or you would not be here today. Procreation is the first element commanded in the original commission. God also allows you to impart identity to your children through naming them. He left room for mankind to have a very real and vital role in the management of the family business. Mankind constantly co-creates with God. New ideas, inventions, art, music, businesses, nations, cultural practices, building, and systems emerge from the authority and power that God has shared with us. He not only loves you, but he loves what you create when you emulate him. God could have done it all himself, but he chose to delegate the authority and responsibility for the governance of creation to his children. God gave you a metron, and he made room for you to matter.

Chapter 10

Welcome To Your Metron

*"We, however, will not boast beyond measure, but within the limits of the **sphere**
[METRON] which God appointed us..."*(2 Corinthians 10:13 NKJV)

THE WORD *SPHERE* IS TRANSLATED FROM THE Greek word *metron*. A metron is
essentially a sphere of influence. What is the actual definition of a metron?
Let's look at the Greek word as used by the Apostle Paul in the scripture.

Definition of the Greek word metron (μέτρον)[9]

1. measure, an instrument for measuring
2. determined extent, portion measured off, measure or limit

The Apostle Paul introduces us to this idea of our metron. He explains
that he has a "measure" or "sphere" of influence that God had given him.
Paul had a metron measured out to him and his ministry. Paul's metron
was the sphere of influence that he was aware of and for which he took
responsibility. He made it clear in his letter to the Corinthians that there
where things and people inside and outside of his metron. Paul also makes
it clear that he is taking his "measured" area of responsibility very seriously.
Through relationship with God, we can discover the area of responsibility
that God has given us. Once we have identified the portion of the kingdom
we have inherited, then we are free to co-labor with Christ in the family
business. *Your metron is essentially the scope of work you do within the Father's
family business.* You matter to all that is within your metron; what you do
with your metron matters to God.

---

9 *Strong's Concordance #G3358*

God designs and assigns every human a metron. Your metron is the context and season in time to which you are called and in which the original commission is carried out through your life. Here is my colloquial definition of a metron.

The metron is a measure of responsibility delegated by God to you in the midst of creation, culture, and spiritual history.

Picture a metron as a portion of creation to which God has commissioned you to influence. Within this sphere of influence is contained aspects of creation, elements of human activity and spiritual activity, and primarily your own self or "being." The concept of a realm is probably more familiar to us as we hear it often used in history, literature, and occasionally in reference to political monarchies. Realm means a "kingdom" or "field or domain of activity or interest."

Within your metron is found the jurisdiction in which you are to co-labor with God during your lifetime on earth. God establishes you in his created order from the day you are born. He has created a place for you to thrive and for your gifts, callings, and identity to be established. Just like Adam and Eve, you were born into a garden, and this garden is your metron. From the moment your eyes are opened both physically and spiritually, you were called to take responsibility for the condition of your metron.

Along with the responsibilities you have received comes the blessing of finding your place in the family of God. What you do with what God has given you matters throughout eternity, starting now. The metron you manage matters in the Kingdom of God. Creation was designed to require mankind to work for it to work. So too, your metron requires your co-laboring with Christ to thrive.

"The greatest issue facing the world today, with all its heartbreaking needs, is whether those who, by profession or culture, are identified as "Christians" will become disciples — students, apprentices, practitioners — of Jesus Christ, steadily learning from him how to live the life of the Kingdom of the Heavens into every corner of human existence." (Dallas Willard)[10]

Your metron is your "corner of human existence." God is thrilled to give you a meaningful role in what he has created. Remember it is God who designs

---

10 *Dallas Willard, The Great Omission: Reclaiming Jesus' Essential Teachings on Discipleship*

and assigns metrons as the context for your good works. Managing your metron becomes the heart of your vocation and the context within which you find purpose.

Chapter 11
Cultivate

LIKE EVERYTHING, THE CONCEPT OF VOCATION ORIGINATED somewhere and at some point in time. To gain a Biblical understanding of labor and vocation within the Kingdom of God, we need to start at the beginning where the first principles for mankind were established.

> *"Then the Lord God took the man and put him into the garden of Eden to **cultivate** it and **keep** it."* (Genesis 2:15, emphasis added)

There are two keywords in this scripture; The first is "cultivate" and the second is "keep." Let's look at the first command given to Adam and Eve — "cultivate." This word comes from the Hebrew word *abad*, and in the text, it means: "cultivate, tend, serve, worship." [11] We should note the first directive from God to mankind is to cultivate or work. *Abad* is also translated as worship. To understand the word used in this scripture for *work*, we need to intentionally let the definitions mingle together to form a holistic understanding of the word *abad*.

We must address one damaging misunderstanding about the idea that one activity is worship or "spiritual" and another is not. There is a gnostic view that segregates human activity into sacred & secular activities, and this has led to the idea that work is not spiritual. The result of this disaster is the loss of dignity and the purpose of vocation. To the depths that we have allowed this compartmentalization of life into "sacred" activities and "secular" activities, we have undermined God's original design. If work is not considered to be a form of worship, it is evidence that we have allowed work to remain under the curse of the fall. We have, in fact, contributed to

---

11 *Strong's Concordance #H5647*

the success of the system that is resisting the Kingdom of God by abdicating our position of spiritual authority in creation. To realign we must redefine.

Colossians 3:23–24 teaches, "Whatever you do, work at it with all your heart, as working for the Lord, not for human masters, since you know that you will receive an inheritance from the Lord as a reward. It is the Lord Christ you are serving."

Work is *worship*. The vast majority of the waking portion of your life is dedicated to working. Work includes all your areas of responsibility and influence, including family, social, and vocational activities. Work is not just what you do to earn money. One does not expect to be paid to worship God. Financial provision through vocation is God's design, but the heart of labor is worship. Anything done in obedience to the Lord and from meaningful intention toward God is worship. The believer who is truly embracing the original commission must not allow a gap between work and worship for both are the same.

"Lord, you alone are my portion and my cup; you make my lot secure. The boundary lines have fallen for me in pleasant places; surely, I have a delightful inheritance."(Psalm 16:5–6)

The mandate to "cultivate," seems to be extremely broad and might be difficult the believer to apply. In actuality, it is simple when you grasp the scriptural idea of "metrons" In Psalm 16 King David refers to the inheritance given him by God as "boundary lines." Your work and influence are given a particular realm that has set borders or boundaries. All that is contained within these borders is what the apostle Paul refers to as your "metron." God has established these borders for our us, and within this realm, the Lord gives us context for our life. Adam and Eve were given the Garden of Eden as their initial sphere of responsibility. All believers also have been given a garden. The apostle Paul indicates that he had a defined metron and I believe that all believers have a similarly defined sphere of influence. Knowing our boundaries gives us security and confidence. Even Paul recognized that some things were not in his metron and yet he took responsibility for that which was included. Paul was called to his sphere, his metron, and you are called to manage your metron.

The Good Work of Vocation

"God is working to reverse the effects of the Fall, and he calls us to work with him."(Darrow Miller)[12]

"What do you do"? This is a common question that we are asked when meeting new people. We all have different answers based on our day to day activities. One might answer that, "I am a student" or, "I work in such and such industry" or, "I'm the mother of 4 children." She might rightly respond that she does four full-time jobs! No matter the season of life we are in or the scope of responsibility that currently describes our metron, we all work for a common company. As followers of Christ, we are all in the family business.

What does the family business do? Our father is in the reconciliation and restoration business, and your collaboration (co-laboring) with him is how he gets business done. Within all our diversity of activity in the family business, we all have a unifying bottom line. We are working with our Father to reverse the effects of the Fall. When we grasp this high calling, our work gets truly exciting, and even work that seems mundane or inconsequential becomes deeply fulfilling.

What you do is not the point. What matters is how you do what you do where you are.

Whether you are a stay at home parent, a bank teller, entrepreneur, or the leader of a nation, the Original Commission imparts authority and responsibility to manage the metron God has given you. Just as in the parable of the Talents in Matthew 25:14, we will be held accountable for how we manage his possessions. God wants you to learn to be faithful with the "little" so that he can entrust you with "much." (Matthew 25:21)

If, by chance, you try to avoid God's design, you might abdicate personal responsibility by saying something like, "I don't have any sort of metron." The truth is that everyone has parents, friends, co-workers, hobbies, social standing, school, vocation, family, property, community, ideas, and dreams. Every metron is a compilation of all of these aspects of life. Your metron may be smaller and simpler to navigate, but it contains at least one distinct project. Everyone has a sphere of influence that at least contains one per-

---

12 *Darrow Miller, LifeWork*

son, you. Your metron is the garden into which you were placed to serve and protect.

The scope and purpose of the original commission resonate in your garden even if you are technically unemployed. In the Kingdom of God, you are always employed in the family business. No matter what you do on a day to day basis, you are commissioned to reverse the effects of the fall within anyone or anything that you can influence. You may not have a "job" but you do have influence. You may not have many resources, but you have at least one of God's "gifts." You may not have employees to manage or citizens to govern, but you do have a metron even if it only contains you! If you look around with a discerning heart you will begin to recognize the many areas of the human condition to which you are connected as a lifeline to heaven.

In the kingdom, work can be defined as any activity to which you set your hand to do. Work is the means through which you establish the Kingdom of God. Vocation is not only a calling to what is immediately at hand to do. It also has eternal significance.

If work is truly a calling and of eternal significance in the Kingdom of God, then why do so many try to avoid it? The problem has to do with our world view of work. We have to answer this question. "Is work in the way, or is it the way?"

To find purpose and calling in our vocation, we must align with God's view of work.

World Views of Work

To know if you are aligned with God's original commission examine your worldview of work. The condition of your metron is an outworking of your thinking. Your thinking is a product of your worldview. Let's examine several distinct worldviews of work as put forward by leading Christian thought leader Darrow Miller. Each perspective will either hinder or enable the completion of our Original Commission.

Animistic worldview regarding work: The distinguishing characteristic of this view is that "work is a necessary evil" that one puts up with in order to have food to eat.

Materialistic Worldview of Work: The distinguishing characteristic of this view is that a person works to succeed and have material wealth.

These first two views are predominant within most cultures around the world. Though work is designed to provide the laborer with food and material gain, Scripture provides us with a much higher view of work. Throughout history, the original design for work in the Kingdom of God has been constantly undermined. A low view of work has emerged as the accepted norm in Christian circles. It has been built on a false dichotomy that views reality as having sacred and secular elements. This sacred and secular delineation is not biblical. It was introduced through the heresy of Gnosticism. Embracing Gnosticism in the body of Christ has allowed for work to be segregated into sacred and secular. A prominent consequence of this false dichotomy regarding work has been the denigration of vocation and the undermining of God's original commission. If work is no longer viewed as worship, then it becomes a secondary activity that is no longer spiritual.

The Denigration of Vocation

What is Gnosticism? It was one of the most prevalent heresies that threatened the early church. Influenced by such philosophers as Plato, Gnosticism is based on two false premises.

1. Matter is inherently evil, and the spirit is inherently good.
2. Everything in (of) the body has no meaning because life only exists in the spirit realm.

To deeply understand why work is so misunderstood in Christianity, we need to touch on the idea of Gnosticism. Gnosticism is a heresy that emerged in the early church and has continued to affect the thinking of believers to this day. The apostle Paul was particularly vocal in his opposition and condemnation of the Gnostics as he sought to disciple the early church. He would not allow the belief that one's actions were not as important as one's spiritual activity. Gnosticism leads to a "dis-integrated" life rather than a holistically managed human existence. A Gnostic worldview allows for the work of one's hands to be of no spiritual significance.

The early church fathers taught against Gnosticism and its destructive influence in the early church. Today we find that it is still alive and well in the modern church. Gnosticism has succeeded in belittling the Biblical understanding of work and allowing for a person's career to be considered secular. This has robbed believers of their sense of purpose and calling. The idea that some things in life are sacred, and some are secular is rooted in Gnosticism and is opposed to a biblical worldview. In the kingdom world-view, everything is integrated. There is no secular activity since everything should be done as worship unto the Lord.

Are you a Christian gnostic?

Consider your world view of work as we explore the concept of "Evangelical Gnostic Paradigms." Darrow Miller puts forward the following concepts in his book *LifeWork*.

First evangelical Gnostic paradigm of work: "The distinguishing characteristic of this view is that there is work that is 'spiritual' and work that is 'secular.' From this perspective, the world and secular jobs are seen as slightly evil, bad, or only necessary. If one wants to be more spiritual, then he or she goes into "full-time Christian service." This is defined as pastoring, missions, and other "spiritual work."

Second Evangelical Gnostic Paradigm of work: "The distinguishing characteristic of this view is that one should endeavor to 'spiritualize' your secular work. Some Christians who do not want to go into "full-time Christian work," seek to invest spiritual activity into their workplace. Attempts are made to validate your work by spiritualizing it through ONLY seeing your workplace as a place to do spiritual ministry."

The great loss of these Gnostic Paradigms is that by embracing a low view of work you have been dislocated from your design. Without a recognition that work is the primary means through which the kingdom has established the value of your vocation is minimized. The Gnostic view of work produces dislocation and denigration of the value of work. Any attack on the redemptive nature of work is an attack on the Kingdom of

God and the very nature of creation. Work must be considered worthy and worshipful in its very nature. Work is not something that is in the way of doing something spiritual or just a context for doing something for God. Work is by its very design spiritual and of eternal significance. As we saw in Genesis, creation was designed to require your participation. You have to work for creation to work.

Darrow Miller goes on to describe the biblical worldview of work as a "framework for work being sacred, for labor having dignity. This concept of work is that it is a vocation—one's calling. Work is a call of God upon an individual's life. It becomes the sphere through which, not merely in which, a Christian serves Christ and his kingdom. It is the occupation—the principal business of one's life—through which one occupies territory or a sphere of influence (Luke 19:13) for Jesus Christ."

Key indicators that you have a kingdom Worldview of Work:

1. Work is spiritual
2. Work is a reflection of the Character and Nature of God
3. Work is the means through which God establishes his kingdom
4. Work is of eternal value
5. Work is an act of worship
6. Work is a vocation or a "calling"
7. Work has inherent dignity and imparts dignity
8. Work is vocation, a calling from God on a person's life
9. Work is God's original design for mankind
10. Work is understood to be vital for the flourishing of creation

Chapter 12
The Garden Model

As with all things that God created, the garden had an original design. The Garden of Eden was designed to be a microcosm example of how creation was to function when all was in alignment with God's design. This microcosm environment provided a context for the relationship between created and creator. As the garden was the original footprint of heaven on earth, it would be wise for us to explore what was actually going on in this environment. Specific details may elude us as there is not a moment by moment account illustrated in scripture, but the overall design is clear. If we take a deeper look at the narrative of the garden I believe what we find has significant implications in our daily lives in the kingdom.

Many of us grew up with what I like to call the "Sunday School" understanding of the Garden of Eden. How many of us were taught by well-intended Sunday school teachers that "if Adam and Eve hadn't sinned, we would all still be lounging around in paradise"? This glossy vision of the pre-sin condition of creation is not accurate, and it surely does not answer the question of "what exactly was going on in the garden?" *The garden was designed as a working model of cultivated creation for mankind to reproduce.* It was a benchmark, not a destination resort. Not only was the garden a model of how creation was to be ordered and managed, but it was also a model of how the relationship with God was to be ordered and managed.

Vertical and Horizontal Cultivation

One of the purposes of the garden was to illustrate to Adam and Eve the "model" environment that was defined by a rightly ordered relationship between Man, God, and Creation. This original design was the blueprint that was to guide their work of fulfilling their commission. Adam and Eve were to reference this design as they cultivated all of creation.

The garden was a place of perfect, unhindered relationship between God and mankind. As mentioned in Genesis 3:8, God would come down and walk in the garden in the cool of the day. This place of right relationship between God and Man is the essence of original design. The model environment of the garden provides us with a vision of the Kingdom of God in its purest form.

In God's garden design, there were two distinct yet integrated relational management aspects. Adam's original commission required attention to both of these. We can describe the first as the vertical relationship between God and Mankind. The vertical was the personal, interactive relationship that Adam and Eve enjoyed with their father, God. We can describe the second aspect of relational management as lateral. This was mankind's horizontal relationship with creation.

Mankind was originally designed to manage both the vertical and horizontal relationships within their garden or sphere of influence. The garden provided an example of what creation would be like when all was in order both spiritually and naturally or vertically and horizontally. Adam and Eve discovered they must *manage up* to *manage out*. When the vertical relationship with God had been broken through sin, it became almost impossible to manage outward into creation. Instead of cultivating creation into the likeness of the garden they ended up cultivating creation under the curse of the fall. They were broken spiritually, and creation was broken naturally. Without the author, humans cannot co-author.

God did not leave mankind and the rest of creation without hope. God's plans and purposes for the restoration of relationship with mankind and the restoration of creation became the arc of spiritual history. This arc started with Adam and Eve and encompasses you even today. The original design for rightly ordered, vertical, and horizontal relationship is still at the heart of the kingdom and the goal of managing your metron. Adam had the garden at the heart of his metron, and we have the model of the garden that teaches us how to manage our metrons.

When Jesus died and was resurrected, the system was rebooted, and God engaged his co-authors to set things right. In the Kingdom of God you are again required to manage up and manage out. The condition of your vertical relationship will inform what you reproduce into your horizontal environment. Just as Adam, you have a metron to manage, and it requires your upward and outward attention.

The Original Connection

The kingdom comes through relationship and is designed for relationship. All things were originally designed to exist in an unhindered relationship with God. His intention of sacred relationship with his people was first manifest in the garden and has continued throughout history to this day.

The garden was the original connection point between heaven and earth, a place where it was likely hard to tell where earth ended and heaven began. To this day, the deepest desire of mankind is to connect with the Divine. To know and be known. Those that do not know the one true God find themselves constantly compelled to find or create their own heaven. The desire for the presence of God is hard-wired into humans, and sadly many are led astray by false gods and human imaginations. The joy and peace that is available to the believer in this life are built on a present relationship with God. We are no longer separated from God but restored to right relationship with him.

When we believed, heaven entered our heart, and we entered heaven. As we read earlier, Colossians 1:13 says we as believers have been transferred into the Kingdom of God. We have been seated in heavenly places in Christ Jesus. God now dwells in your heart through the residing presence of the Holy Spirit. Relationship with the creator is the desire of all mankind and is often referred to as a "God-shaped hole in our heart." As a believer in Christ, your relationship with God is designed to be a lifeline that extends to earth from your seat in heaven. This lifeline extends from where you are seated in heavenly places with Christ to your metron on earth. Just as the garden was a connection point between heaven and earth, your metron also is designed to be connected with heaven. You function as a lifeline as you stand in two realms at the same time. This is the mystery of the Kingdom of God that is now and yet still coming in its fullness.

In Matthew 6:10, Jesus prayed, "Your kingdom come. Your will be done, On earth as it is in heaven." In this example of how his disciples should pray, he was giving direction to our quest to connect.

When we long for heaven, we are truly longing for what Adam and Eve had in the garden, the presence of God. When Jesus taught his disciples to pray, "Your kingdom come your will be done on earth as it is in heaven" he must have been filled with joy knowing that through his pending sacrifice, relationship with his family would again be unhindered. The original design would be restored.

In the garden model, we see that the creator was in charge but he was ruling through unhindered relationship with his people. Adam and Eve were given the original commission by the King and made responsible for that kingdom. They had the privilege of co-laboring with their Father God and what they did or did not do truly mattered to eternity. Their choices surely mattered in the epic story of creation and mankind. As children of God, our choices still matter, and the "Original Commission" still stands.

On Earth, as it is in Heaven

What do we see when we look deeply into the Original Commission? We see that the garden was a living example of creation under God's perfect rule and reign, managed by his image-bearing children. The whole earth was intended to become like the garden, a place defined by the presence of God and a context of unhindered relationship with his people. Adam and Eve were privileged to be the first to receive the original commission and the first to experience the joy of co-laboring with God to cultivate creation.

A curious aspect of the creation narrative is the description of creation outside the garden. This part of creation required subjugation through work or cultivation. Conditions outside the garden, both spiritual and natural, were not necessarily the same as inside the garden. The original commission was not a suggested, recreational activity to give mankind something to keep them busy.

It was a way of doing life, according to God's original design. Creation was waiting for God's children to take charge and cultivate its potential. As the story of creation and the fall of mankind unfolds, it becomes apparent that Satan was already on the earth. He had some degree of freedom to influence and that influence on Adam and Eve is still felt today. We live in a fallen world, but within this world, we are seeking to reverse the effects of the fall. Now that Jesus has taken back all authority and paid the price for every sin, we can co-labor with God to reconnect creation with its creator. Once you are saved then you are called to work. Reconciliation and restoration are the work of the believer, and the metron you have received is the context for your work.

Instructions were given, and authority was granted to spread out, fill the earth, and subdue it. Adam and Eve were given the responsibility of reproducing the beauty, order and the atmosphere of the garden into that which was outside of the garden. They were commissioned as co-laborers who were themselves created to be image-bearers of their creator. They were to reproduce who they were into creation and fill the earth with the same unbroken relationship with God that was modeled in the garden. This vision for subduing would have imparted an immense sense of purpose to Adam and Eve. The trust that God placed in them would have brought identity, peace, and confidence.

Through the work of cultivation, Adam was to advance the footprint of the garden.

Adam and Eve had perfect context and a clear purpose for their existence. They were to reach out and cultivate the areas of creation that lay outside of the garden. Through the means of work, they were steadily to bring those natural areas into order. The ordering of the natural depended on the ordering of the spiritual. *The only way that the original commission could be carried out was if relationship with God was well-managed upward.* Adam and Eve were responsible to cultivate and steward their upward relationship with God, and to cultivate the world around them.

Mankind was always designed to manage up and manage out. *We have a vertical responsibility to our creator and a lateral responsibility for creation.* As Adam and Eve discovered after their fall, if either goes unmanaged, then the other is also broken. The garden was a model of perfect vertical and horizontal relationship—a holistic human existence. *A right relationship with God turns all of mankind's labors into connection points with heaven.* Adam and Eve found themselves working to cultivate and steward the garden.

They were trusted by God to subdue new territory and cultivate it into the likeness of the garden. The garden was essentially a blueprint of what all of creation was to look like once it was subdued. The garden was a benchmark example. Adam and Eve were not only managing the natural aspects of creation. They were also managing the creation's spiritual dynamics. Their work of cultivating and stewarding was relevant in both the spiritual and natural realms. They managed their vertical relationship with God, and God gave them the authority to manage creation laterally.

When their upward relationship was broken, they lost the authority to manage outwards. Spiritual authority originates with God and flows down to his people. It is delegated. The great loss at the fall was the undermining of the entire original design. The whole of creation was to be successfully cultivated and subdued by mankind, but this commission depended on delegated authority. The design was for creation to be permeated by the atmosphere of the presence of God. Creation was originally designed to be naturally supernatural. In the beginning, conditions were truly on earth as they were in heaven. Adam and Eve found themselves centrally positioned and entrusted with an epic project, a project that depended on work. The question is, what were they actually doing in their metron?

Chapter 13
Culture Matters

THE AUTHOR OF THE BOOK *LifeWork* AND Christian worldview thought leader, Darrow Miller, says, "Culture is where the spiritual and the natural come together."

I want to illustrate in the following section that *culture is a by-product of worship, and that culture is fundamentally spiritual.* The essence of God's original design was that mankind would be responsible for cultivating the culture of heaven into the earth through fulfilling the Original Commission. As we saw earlier in this study, just as Adam and Eve, we are also given a garden, or a "metron" into which we are commissioned to cultivate and keep.

The formation and management of culture is the ultimate aim of the original commission. Worship is how culture is established, and work is the primary form of worship. Before we get to the cultural aspect of this study, we have to build the framework on which our relationship to culture can be understood. Let's start with the mandate to work.

Work (labor) is why Adam was placed into his garden and why you are also placed into your metron. This sovereign arrangement imparted purpose to mankind at the beginning, and this original design still defines us today. Our original commission is initially activated by God when he places Adam into his position of authority and responsibility in the garden. Adam and by extension, mankind, are given the commission to cultivate, expand and keep what God had established.

Mankind was given responsibility and given authority to fulfill his calling. At the time Adam and Eve receive the original commission they also receive authority over creation described metaphorically as keys. The keys or the "delegated authority" was the prize that Satan intensely desired.

It appears Satan (Lucifer) wanted to be like God and attempted to assert himself against God's authority. It did not go well for him or his followers. Instead of becoming the ruler, he suddenly finds himself being subjugated by little image-bearers of God! God would never allow his authority to be taken — but he willingly shared it with mankind. The only way the enemy could get access to that authority was to get mankind to give it to him. Thus Adam and Eve became targets in Satan's hostile takeover attempt.

By disobeying God and choosing to sin, Adam and Eve yielded to Satan. Mankind submitted their God-given authority to the very one who intended to corrupt all that God had designed. Mankind found themselves in slavery to sin, and the nature of work went from joy to misery. By the grace of God, we have been set free through faith in Jesus and repentance from sin. Christ's work at the cross ended up restoring our authority over creation and inaugurating the Kingdom of God.

Work was redeemed from the curse of the fall, and we have reclaimed our original design. Work is no longer under a curse though all of creation still suffers under the effects of the fall. In the kingdom that has come and is still to come the very nature of work is restored. Satan has been defeated, and every curse has been broken. Now that Jesus has defeated the powers of darkness and taken back all authority in heaven and on earth, you are free, and your work is a means of bringing freedom to your metron.

Bringing freedom from the effects of the fall is the business of every believer. Restoration of mankind's vertical relationship with God and a horizontal relationship with creation were made possible by the cross. Jesus beautifully outmaneuvered the enemy of our souls and graciously continued his original plan for mankind. The original commission was back in business!

Through salvation, we are now free to obey and fulfill the original commission. Under the new covenant, we have been liberated from subjugation to sin and the curse. The sacrifice of Jesus reconciles and restores all who believe and repent. Through the death and resurrection of Christ, God's original design is at work again; the garden is back! We are re-commissioned with the original commission to see his kingdom come and his will be done, on earth as it is in heaven, starting with your metron!

The First Element of Vocation

"Then the Lord God took the man and put him into the garden of Eden to culti-vate [abad / avad] it and keep it."(Genesis 2:15)

I propose that two distinct "elements" related to work or vocation are found in Genesis 2: The first element of vocation indicated is the word cultivate, or *abad* in the original text. The second element of vocation we see included is the word "keep." We will look closely at the word "keep" later in this study, but initially, we must explore the first element of vocation and the nature of mankind's first job.

Work as Worship

What was Adam actually supposed to do when God gave him the original commission? What was meant by cultivate? To discover our purpose, we need to explore the mandate to cultivate. Work was designed to be worship. This foundational concept is vital to this effort to construct a theological framework for vocation. If a vocation is to be meaningful and work eternal then it must be fundamentally spiritual. When labor is done in the physical realm as unto the Lord it takes on a spiritual dimension as does any act of worship.

Worship is designed to make its way to the presence of God and attract the presence of God to that worship. When work is done as worship, it cultivates the spiritual atmosphere and attracts the presence of God into your metron. Labor done worshipfully and for the glory of God is set free from the effects of the fall. It becomes a joy and not a curse. Labor done under the wrong worldview and not directed to the Lord as worship remains subject to the curse. Labor devoid of worship causes the worker to suffer and creation to languish. If labor is done as worship it will not only accomplish its natural design, but it will accomplish God's purposes in the spiritual realm.

As we explored in the previous section on the Theology of Work, the word "cultivate" is from the Hebrew word *abad*. It literally means to "cultivate, tend, serve, worship."

Two distinct but connected elements are contained in the command to *abad*.

The first element is the physical stewardship of the garden. Adam, and by implication mankind, was commissioned to steward and manage the physical condition of creation. The garden was to be tended and maintained both physically and spiritually. The garden was designed to be a residence of God as well as man. In fact, it was the temple where God and men first communed. Your metron is also a garden that God designed to function as a temple. God desires to reside in you as you reside in your metron. He enjoys you, and he enjoys his creation. Through you, the metron manager, he wants to bless everything that you influence.

The work of physically maintaining and improving the condition of creation is a commission from God and part of mankind's original design. All obedience is a form of worship. The activity of cultivation is obedience and inherently a form of worship. Adam's obedience to cultivate became his primary means of worship. Stewardship and physical labor are clearly sacred, but there is another dimension to the word *abad* that we need to consider. Work was designed for more than just an activity to keep mankind busy. Work becomes what it was meant to be when it is done as worship.

Humans will take on the attributes of whatever we worship. That which is worshiped shapes the worshiper. Then the world around us begins to look like the world inside of us. This is the nature of influence. Influence is the outward effect of your inner reality on the world around you. To manage your metron well, learn to understand how influence is managed. You were commissioned to influence — for better or worse.

The purpose of the garden is also the purpose of your metron. If you are to properly manage your metron, you need to know what you are actually supposed to do. To understand the spiritual roots of the mandate to cultivate, we must explore the deeper dimension of the word *abad* (cultivate).

Avad = Worship

The word *avad* or *abad* in the Hebrew text meant the "work of cultivation." Understanding the translation of this word is crucial to our study. The origin of the English language word cultivate has descended from the Latin word *cultus*.

"Cultus is often translated as 'cult' without the negative connotations the word may have in English, or with the Old English word 'worship,' but it implies the necessity of active maintenance beyond passive adoration."[13]

In addition to the act of tilling or cultivating, one of the primary meanings of the word *cultus* is the act of honoring or worshiping, reverence, adoration, veneration; loyalty. Another linguistic descendant of *cultus* is the Spanish word *cultos*, which means worship. Or in popular translation "a worship service."

We can see that a deeper aspect of the word cultivate is the concept of worship. The definition of the word cultivate not only pointed towards physical stewardship or tending and serving but also points to the crux of the commission, worship. The equal use of the word cultivate to describe physical work, and spiritual worship expresses the core understanding that the purpose of work is worship. The purpose of your vocation and the activities to which you were called are, in fact, spiritual by design. Adam's physical stewardship and labor were a form of worship to God, but we also see that Adam was cultivating or "tending" another dimension of the garden.

Adam and Eve were commissioned to *actively* steward and maintain the environment that existed in the garden. One of unhindered relationship with the creator. This was where God and man walked and talked together in the perfect original design. The garden was not only a perfect physical environment in which mankind would thrive. It was also a perfect spiritual environment where relationship with God would exist in perfection. It was literally heaven on earth. The deeper element of Adam's original commission was that he would steward, tend, and serve in such a way as to maintain relationship with God through cultivating an environment of worship. As we saw in the earlier definition of the word *cultus*, this was something to be actively maintained. Cultivation is active and not a passive mandate.

In Matthew 6:10, Jesus prayed, "Your kingdom come. Your will be done, On earth as it is in heaven."

With the backdrop of the cultivation narrative, this section of the Lord's Prayer takes on a different dimension. There once was a time when God's

---

13 *Ando, The Matter of the Gods, pp. 5–7; Valerie M. Warrior, Roman Religion (Cambridge University Press, 2006), p. 6; James B. Rives, Religion in the Roman Empire (Blackwell, 2007), pp. 13, 23.*

will was done on earth as it was in heaven. It was in the garden, before the fall of man. Jesus was praying "let it be as it once was." His heart for restoration and reconciliation with mankind was again evidenced through his instructional prayer.

Mankind, through Adam, was given the responsibility to actively cultivate the model environment of physical perfection and spiritual perfection. The spiritual order that was the fruit of a right relationship with God enabled Adam to reproduce right order in the natural world. This was the first example of the principle that the natural world you influence is designed to resemble the spiritual reality inside you.

G.K. Beale addresses this dynamic in his book *The Temple and the Church's Mission*. He says, "...Adam was much more than a gardener but was to maintain the created order of the sacred space of the sanctuary." He goes on to say that "Adam's priestly role in the garden was to 'manage' or 'care' for it by maintaining its order and keeping out 'uncleanness.' This included 'gardening' but likely went beyond it to managing the affairs of the sacred place where God's presence dwelt and maintain its orderliness in contrast to the disordered space outside."[14]

Adam was to physically and spiritually cultivate the garden and actively subdue the creation that was outside the garden. Adam and Eve had a job description that encompassed both spiritual and natural dynamics. They were not just pruning trees and clearing up rivers. They were cultivating and stewarding an environment that hosted the presence and person of God.

The garden was the working model of God's design for creation. Adam was given an example by which he could measure success as he carried out the original commission. If the spiritual and natural conditions outside the garden were in the same condition as inside the garden, then he was succeeding. Adam and Eve had a God-sized responsibility and could only carry it out through an unbroken relationship with God. That position was lost through the fall, but in Christ our position is restored. Our relationship with God has now been restored through the cross, and we can carry out our God-sized commission.

The garden was the original manifestation of the Kingdom of God on earth. It was the touch-point of heaven and earth. God intended to rule and reign through co-laboring with mankind. Mankind was commissioned

---

14 *G.K. Beale The Temple and the Church's Mission, Page 84–85*

to steward and subdue the creation of the King. Key to fulfilling that commission was to cultivate. All of the descendants of Adam and Eve have the same "Original Commission," and all have a "metron" to manage.

The Roots of Culture

The English word Culture descends from the Latin word *cultus*. As we have observed previously, the Latin word *cultus* means "worship"/"work."

Part of their original commission was to cultivate relationship with God through worshipful work. Adam and Eve were commissioned not only for creation care but also to determine what "spiritual software" would operate on "God's hardware." They were the original culture shapers. Thus we find that what the heart of the original commission was truly about was maintaining and expanding the holistic culture of the garden. The culture of the garden was a product of perfect vertical and horizontal relationship between God, mankind, and creation.

Adam and Eve held hands with God and kept their feet in their garden. Scripture describes the garden environment as the place where God would come down and walk in the garden in the cool of the day. Indeed God is often referred to in scripture as "the God who comes down."

Culture is Supernatural

Culture is what everything is about, but what is it? Why does it exist? Why does it matter? How does it form? Culture is ultimately a manifestation of spiritual realities interwoven with the context of the natural world. It is a system that is informed by whomever mankind worships. For better or worse.

We must understand that the universal pillars of what we know as "culture" are supernatural in origin. If not, then we are doomed to drown in the superficial manifestations of much deeper realities. All of the confusion, strife, and misery that the cultures of the world regularly encounter are easily understood if we maintain a spiritual paradigm. Culture is fundamentally a manifestation of spiritual realities embraced by a people.

Cultural landscapes are manifestations of a vertical relationship with the "gods." When mankind has been deceived and led into relationship with false gods, they re-empower a disempowered devil. We enable what we worship because we are authorized to use our God-given authority to shape creation for better or worse.

People worship what they value. Sadly, mankind often values what the enemy of our souls has to offer, over and above what God has commissioned. Culture is the ultimate battleground where values collide, and the character and nature of the one true living God and his enemies are revealed. This is the landscape of life and death and where trees are judged by their fruit (Luke 6:43–44).

People cultivate that which they value. The original commission empowers mankind for good or evil because God has not withdrawn his delegated authority even when people or spirits rebel. People have the power and authority to cultivate the garden of their metron for better or worse. What they cultivate either establishes the culture of the Kingdom of God or the culture of the kingdom of this world. Ultimately, we are all actively participating in writing the software code that will manage our metron. We are writing code constantly, and we don't do it on our own. The code we are producing is co-authored with either the spirit of God or by the spirit of the enemy.

Kingdom and Culture

The heart of the original commission is that your metron would be constantly reformed and renewed as you embrace of the King of Kings and Lord of Lords. When you stand on earth and hold on to heaven, you become a conduit for the culture found in heaven to flow into the garden of earth. The first evidence of this heavenly inflow is that your inner man is reborn and the second indicator is that your metron begins to glow with the presence of God. *Culture is designed to be the primary visible example of the presence of God.*

In the Gospel of Luke, the Kingdom of God is illustrated. It is planted in a man's garden and cultivated.

"So he was saying, "Then Jesus asked, "What is the Kingdom of God like? What shall I compare it to? It is like a mustard seed, which a man took and planted in his garden. It grew and became a tree, and the birds perched in its branches." (Luke 13:18–19)

In this scripture, we see that the man laid hold of the kingdom and planted it in his garden or, his metron. This metron is his sphere of influence. Where he was cultivating or working. This kingdom seed grew and became a tree that provided for the well being of creation beyond itself.

The values of the kingdom are designed to shape the creation of culture. The parables are examples that Jesus used to describe the Kingdom of God as influencing and shaping reality. Look at this scripture through the lens of culture-shaping as Jesus describes the Kingdom of God in Luke 13:20–2. "Again he asked, 'What shall I compare the Kingdom of God to? It is like yeast that a woman took and mixed into about sixty pounds of flour until it worked all through the dough.'"

The Kingdom of God is described here as a tiny element of influence that is introduced into a huge amount of flour. Through the woman's "work" it was mixed in and transformed the flour into something that would provide wellbeing and sustenance. Both the mustard seed and the yeast are created by God but require the "work" or cultivation by mankind to produce fruit.

If you want to fulfill your original commission and see the culture of heaven established in your metron, apply this simple equation:

$$Seed + God + Mankind \times Cultivation = Kingdom.$$

Seed = Creation
God = Authority, Author, and Creator
Mankind = Co Laborer, Co-Author
Cultivation = Work and Vocation
Kingdom = Transformed, Fruitful and Subdued

Chapter 14
The Formation of Culture

It is helpful for any discussion of a concept to start by clarifying terms. The simple definition of the word *culture* is the behaviors and beliefs characteristic of a particular social, ethnic, or age group.

This is a reasonable definition of explicit culture or the visible top-level of culture that can be readily seen or experienced by an observer. There are also vast and often convoluted underlying histories and structures that support the top-level of a given culture. These are often known as deep culture, primary culture, or implicit culture. Culture is a complicated matter, and there are vast amounts of study dedicated to unraveling the mysteries and formation of culture. What we are exploring here is the deepest foundation.

The point of origin for any culture is found in its primary allegiances to spiritual entities and the rituals of relationship with those entities that have emerged. If we can avoid being drowned in the ocean of opinions found in the many studies of culture and keep a supernatural perspective, we can truly understand why things are the way they are. Culture matters since the interrelationship of humans and supernatural beings matters. Culture hinges on the worshiped and the worshiper.

Let's clarify what culture is and is not to help guide our discussion.

A simple definition of Culture:
"patterns of accepted behavior, and the beliefs and values that promote and reinforce them."

Culture is:
- Understood as "behaviors, beliefs and characteristics and practices" of a people
- Changeable, malleable and flexible

- Acquired and informed by histories, context, and worldview structures
- Ultimately supernatural

Culture is not:
- Ethnically determined
- Linguistically determined
- Biologically inherited
- Morally neutral (every aspect of culture comes from somewhere and means something)

Culture exists as a function of God's original design. It was designed to be the mechanism through which our identity in the family of God was validated. Culture was also intended to testify of the beauty and order that could be found when God's original design is realized. God designed culture to be the system by which mankind could manifest the realities of heaven into the context of creation.

Culture can be viewed as a coding system or software language by which creation would ultimately be conformed to God's will and led into its highest condition. *The purpose of this system was to teach the world the language of heaven for the benefit of earth.* The foundation of this spiritual or "high" view of culture is the recognition that culture is ultimately supernatural at its very foundation, for good or evil. *Culture is the imprint that is left in a people by whatever they worship.* God's original design was a system by which mankind was intended to align creation with the creator and govern creation according to God's Ways.

A High View of Culture

I refer to the supernatural paradigm of culture as a "High View." The supernatural aspect of culture is often not immediately visible to the observer as it requires the observer to be spiritually, earthly-minded. Even within the body of Christ, most believers do not intuitively see the spiritual nature of culture. Part of our quest as co-laborers with Christ is learning to recognize the "coding" or "culture" that is authored by father God and discern whether that coding or culture is malicious. One question to ask yourself: "Can I look around my sphere of influence and discover who authored it's code and formed the operating system governing my metron?"

Simply stated, the high view of culture recognizes that *culture is the co-authored "software" that* guides mankind. High culture is a manifestation of the human relationship with the divine. *Culture exists because worship exists.* We worship because we have beliefs, we have beliefs because there are many so-called "gods" as the apostle Paul stated in 1st Corinthians 8:5.

What Adam had beheld in the garden was the perfect model of a high functioning relationship between God and his creation. *This relationally ordered reality (on earth as it is in heaven) produced the perfect "software" to program God's hardware (creation).* The software of the garden was the first manifestation of "high culture." The garden was a living example of what the culture of heaven produced when it touched earth. The culture of the garden was a unique example of what creation was like when the presence of God defined the environment. This distinctive condition in the garden was defined by perfectly aligned relationship between the creator and his creation.

What you cultivate radiates

In the beginning, Adam (mankind) was given the original commission to cultivate (subdue) creation. Culture was originally the mechanism that God designed through which mankind would order and steward creation. God's original design was that Adam would reproduce in creation the culture that he had beheld in the garden.

Understanding the truly supernatural nature of culture will enable believers to understand their role as co-laborers and co-authors with God. Your original commission was the same as Adam's original commission; you are to radiate the presence of God and transform creation through cultivation. Adam's original commission was to cultivate and protect culture because culture is truly significant.

A Low View of Culture

It is helpful to clarify at this point that there is also a *low* view or dimension to culture. As opposed to the *high culture* that is informed by the worship of God and a relationship with his supernatural, *low culture is just a shadow of other spiritual realities.* Much like the shadow of a cloud that is passing in front of the sunlight, low culture is just a coloring or shading found in everyday life. Some examples of low culture would be a person or a people's preferences such as food, clothing styles, entertainment, and other day to day preferences and customs. These routine areas of culture are essentially shadows or reflections of what is established through its beliefs, values, and worship.

In a curiously systematic way, what is embraced at a low culture level floats up as "worship" and reinforces the software of high culture. In this ecosystem of cultural formation, we find that what is valued in low aspects of culture functionally reinforce high culture. We worship what we value and worship shapes culture. This is why all choices matter.

This ecosystem of cultural formation again illustrates that mankind's choices are consequential in the cultural equation. An encouraging dynamic that comes to light is that culture is inherently shapable and changeable.

"Cultures and their Worldviews are better seen as organic, ever-changing systems rather than as static, harmonious systems in which change is bad." (Paul Hiebert)[15]

One is not a prisoner to culture.

A person does not have to have a life determined by some external cultural software. Nor does a nation or people group need to remain locked in a fallen and flawed system that is out of alignment with the ways of God. *You are designed to align with heaven.* You are not a victim of your circumstances or bound to a cultural identity by birth. You are free to co-author your cultural software by altering what you value and what you worship. You and your culture will become like what you worship.

As we are exploring the concept that culture is a byproduct of worship, we should look at the definition of the word "worship."

The Merriam Webster dictionary describes the meaning of worship as:

1. reverence offered a divine being or supernatural power
2. an act of expressing such reverence

---

15 *Paul Hiebert, "Transforming Worldviews" page 46*

3. a form of religious practice with its creed and ritual
4. extravagant respect or admiration for or devotion to an object of esteem

Worship is the act of ascribing and recognizing value in someone or something.

Both High Culture and its shadow, Low Culture, are an outward manifestation of what is worshiped or valued inwardly.

If we are truly to understand the nature and purpose of culture, we have to approach it supernaturally. Culture is authored or "coded" by human beliefs, practices, and preferences. Human agents are coding culture and are always inspired by supernatural entities, knowingly or not. These agents are emulating the ways of the one being worshiped and manifesting the ways of that god back into creation. Human worship either reinforces the ways of the one true living God or the fallen "would-be" gods who are intent on diverting worship to themselves.

The Software of Culture

If we understand culture to be a byproduct of worship, then using the analogy of software to helps us better picture the nature and function of culture. Just as software determines the functioning of computer hardware, so too culture determines the activities that define a metron.

We can picture culture as software that humans co-author to operate the hardware or platform of God's universe. The combining of this code and God's hardware create a *system* that is our day to day reality. *This system is the realm of our metrons.* The mission of the original commission is to make sure that the code we use to cultivate our metron is written in the programming language of heaven.

To manage your metron, you have to code in the right language. If you do things God's way in God's universe, you will see blessing in your own life and the metron entrusted to you. The art of managing your metron is to start with the right source code and through your co-authoring ensure that its cultural system is operating on earth as things are in heaven. Is this an impossible vision? No. I believe it is God's original design.

"Jesus looked at them and said, 'With man this is impossible, but with God all things are possible.'"(Matthew 19:26)

You may or may not be called to *change the world* in a way that would impress the world, but you are called and commissioned to impact your metron in a way that impresses God. An impressive scope or worldly high profile is not what God values. He values relational faithfulness and loyalty to his ways.

God designed the perfect hardware but he gives us the authority and power to co-author the software that runs on his hardware. The software that is written by our beliefs, practices, and preferences create culture. Like any corrupted, badly written software eventually fails to function and can damage hardware; a corrupted culture eventually fails to sustain a people. Only the culture of heaven functions smoothly on God's hardware. The counterfeit culture rendered by sinful men and their idols ultimately fails.

The beauty of God's original design is that change is possible! Cultures can change! Part of the gospel, which means "good news," is that you can be transformed by the renewing of your mind.

"And do not be conformed to this world, but be transformed by the renewing of your mind, so that you may prove what the will of God is, that which is good and acceptable and perfect."(Romans 12:2)

The good news is that you do not need to live as a captive of culture and that culture can be beautifully reformed and freed from the corrupting software of worldliness.

"For you know that it was not with perishable things such as silver or gold that you were redeemed from the empty way of life handed down to you from your ancestors."(1st Peter 1:18)

All men and all cultures are the products of the "empty way of life handed down from our ancestors." The good news (Gospel) is that when we are redeemed or ransomed by Christ fullness of life can be achieved, and hope can be restored. The culture that is overflowing with inspired and redeemed men and women can raise the level of joy and righteousness to such a height that you can feel like the shores of heaven have arrived at the edge of earth.

"Taste and see that the Lord is good; blessed is the one who takes refuge in him." (Psalm 34:8)

The Psalmist exhorts those that seek the Lord not to miss the blessings that come through encountering the presence of the Lord.

The greatest loss a person or a culture can experience is never to have tasted of the goodness of the Lord in the land of the living.

You Become What You Behold

"You become like what you worship. When you gaze in awe, admiration, and wonder at something or someone, you begin to take on something of the character of the object of your worship." (N.T. Wright)[16]

You become what you behold.
You look like what you worship.
You reproduce what you cultivate.

You were designed to look like your heavenly father. Naturally, children resemble their biological parents. Supernaturally, God's children begin to look like him. Transformation is the process that the Apostle Paul indicates is at work as we *behold* the glory of the Lord.

"But we all, with unveiled face, beholding as in a mirror the glory of the Lord, are being transformed into the same image from glory to glory, just as from the Lord, the Spirit." (2 Corinthians 3:18)

Those that behold the Lord are being transformed into his image. The more we behold, the more we become. What does it mean to behold? Behold means to gaze, observe, or fixate on something or someone, especially something remarkable or impressive.

In the Old Testament, there are clear statements about this process of becoming like what we behold.

"They worshiped worthless idols, only to become worthless themselves." (Jeremiah 2:5)

---

16 *N.T.Wright, Simply Christian:Why Christianity Makes Sense*

"Those who make them will become like them, everyone who trusts in them."
(Psalm 115:8)

God's original design was for mankind to be image-bearers of the heavenly Father and reflect his image into all of creation. This is the original function of the system we call culture. This system was intended to allow God to permeate all of creation visibly by radiating through his created children. The process was simple. Through ascribing ultimate value to God, one would worship him, behold him and become like him.

The redemptive aim of this process is that mankind would gaze on the beauty of the Lord and would through this intimate relationship be transformed into the likeness of his creator. God wanted his children to look like him, and he wanted to be manifest through them to all creation.

The original design that God intended was that the inner reality of mankind would be shaped into the perfect likeness of their father through beholding God.

There are questions we often fail to ask. "Why are things the way they are?" "Why is my culture so misguided?" "Why does the condition of my metron look closer to the conditions of hell rather than the culture of heaven?" The central issue is actually "What am I beholding?" The answer to this question, when viewed honestly, will give understanding about why things are the way they are.

These principles will guide the formation of culture within your metron:

1. You become like what you behold.
2. What you worship becomes the source of culture in your metron.
3. The world around you looks like the world inside you.

These principles of cultural formation remind that what happens in your soul is entirely meaningful. Your inner world ultimately defines your outer world. God's original design was for good and not for harm. You are designed to behold him and radiate his ways into your metron. This is how you can see his kingdom established.

Chapter 15

Ruin or Restoration

"What we revere we resemble, either for ruin or restoration." (G.K. Beal)[17]

THE PROCESS OF BEHOLDING AND BECOMING IS part of God's original design. That capability also carries with it a risk factor. Through beholding the Lord, we are transformed into his image, but if we behold and value something *other*, we will become like that upon which we gaze. The mechanism of transformation is just that, a system that God designed. As such, it can be repurposed away from its original intended use and hijacked by the enemy. Satan has used this to tempt mankind to take their eyes off of God and on to him.

When we are lured away and deceived into worshiping idols of any kind, the enemy has successfully found a lens through which he can radiate into your metron. This was Satan's original play in the Garden of Eden when he deceived Adam and Eve. He wanted them to listen to him and doubt God. The ongoing struggle seen throughout scripture and in which we find ourselves involved is the struggle for who will be worshiped. Who will mankind value? Who will mankind behold? Who will mankind resemble? Whose presence will we radiate into our metrons? What will shape the inner man? How will the metron's culture look once mankind has become what they have beheld? Which kingdom do you see when you are honest about the condition of your metron?

Adam and Eve were originally commissioned to expand the heavenly reality of the garden outward into the rest of creation. They could do this because heaven was already in their hearts through a right relationship with their Father God. They walked with God each day. What they beheld in the garden they became. What they became shaped all that they had influence

---

17 *We Become What We Worship; page 311*

over. By design, they were intended to cultivate heaven into earth, but they ended up sowing sin and destruction into their world.

Adam and Eve believed and beheld another god rather than the one true creator. Then corrupted software was introduced into God's perfect hardware through the people who had the password to the system. Satan is like a virus constantly looking for a way to infect a new host. He couldn't get into Adam's metron unless given access and sadly, Adam and Eve willingly handed over the password.

The enemy relies on this same mechanism of beholding and becoming to manifest his will in creation. Culture is the stage where Satan constantly stands up to restate his prideful ambition to "be like God." He desires to see his kingdom come and his own will be done on earth as he wishes it would have been done in heaven. Since he cannot assert his will in heaven, he seeks to deceive mankind and use them to help him rewrite the system according to his will. In his pride, the enemy believes that the code he writes is as good or better than God's.

The lie he wants you to believe is that if you do things his way in God's universe, he will give you everything you want. Like he tempted Christ in the wilderness, he says to you, "All this I will give you if you will bow down and worship me." The incentive he adds to his deception is that "I will give you it all with no accountability and no consequences if you install my code on God's hardware." In truth, the enemy's code only produces failed humans, failed states, and failed cultures. He is the ultimate hacker. His software is designed to kill, steal, and destroy. We must constantly check our metron's condition for vulnerabilities and corrupted code. Part of our original commission is to manage the metron by scanning for viruses. Fixing your eyes constantly on the one true living God imprints on your soul familiarity with the perfect. Through the process of beholding the author of righteousness, we easily detect corrupted code. Your metron is like a computer system, and you are commissioned to identify any code that is not co-authored with heaven.

"For you were formerly darkness, but now you are Light in the Lord; walk as children of Light (for the fruit of the Light consists in all goodness and righteousness and truth), trying to learn what is pleasing to the Lord. Do not participate in the unfruitful deeds of darkness, but instead even **expose them.***"* (Ephesians 5:8–11, emphasis added)

Any personal, corporate, or national culture that shows characteristics which align with the wrong kingdom are to be exposed.

Taking personal responsibility for the condition of culture is a day to day responsibility if you are to cultivate the culture of heaven into every dark corner of your metron.

Idolatry Matters

"…whatever your heart clings to and relies upon, that is your God; trust and faith of the heart alone make both God and idol…"(Martin Luther)

"You shall have no other God before Me."(Exodus 20:3)

Why are the scriptures filled with statements and judgments by God against Idolatry? Idolatry is a clear example of the corruption of the God-ordained mechanism by which his people would become like him. When mankind is lured into gazing on an idol, any idol, they are transformed into the image and likeness that which they behold. God wants us to gaze on him alone. Taking on his characteristics, not the characteristics of false gods. Our Father's hatred of idolatry is a manifestation of his parental defense of his children. He does not want anything or any god to take the place of the one true Father on the throne of our hearts. From a motivation of love and protection, God contends with idols and condemns idolatry. He will not tolerate false gods in our lives. He knows that we will become like what we behold, and the creation around us will be *cultivated* according to the worship of our hearts. The world around us looks like the world inside us. Culture is just a manifestation of the god that is on the throne of our heart.

Culture is significant because culture is a matter of worship and worship is a matter of relationship to the spiritual. A person's or people's behaviors, beliefs, and values are shaped by worship and are the foundations that inform culture. Defining *cultivate* as *worship* is vital because worship determines destiny.

"If it is disagreeable in your sight to serve the Lord, choose for yourselves today whom you will serve: whether the gods which your fathers served which were

beyond the river, or the gods of the Amorites in whose land you are living; but as for me and my house, we will serve the Lord." (Joshua 24:15)

In the famous story of ancient Israel's wilderness wandering and later conquest of the promised land, we see a defining challenge given to the people by their leader Joshua. Joshua is laying out a challenge for the people to choose their god and thus choose their culture and their fate. Joshua rightly says, "But as for me and my house, we will serve the Lord."

Joshua does not deny there are other gods with a legal claim to various geographies and spheres of influence. He only challenges Israel to choose whom they will serve. He gives them the opportunity to choose false gods or the one true God.

Every day as believers, we face this same choice. Which god will we serve? What culture will be manifest in our house? Where will we source the software for our metron? How will the world around us appear? No humans can avoid these choices. Daily, people decide what the world around them will be. The ripple effects of simple, mundane decisions often have spiritual ramifications as important as complex life choices. In truth, there are no meaningless choices; everything has a spiritual dimension and everything matters.

The potential result of walking after something is that you might one day catch up to it. This is the way culture is formed, and destiny determined. As theologian G.K. Beal says in his study on idolatry, "What we revere we resemble, either for ruin or restoration."

Culture is not neutral. Look at what Christ said in Matthew 12:30 "He who is not with Me is against Me, and he who does not gather with Me scatters." Jesus doesn't make room for neutrality in the context of human belief and behavior. We are constantly reinforcing one system or the other — either gathering with the Kingdom of God or scattering through worldliness.

David F. Wells gives us a useful definition of worldliness in his book *God in the Wasteland*.[18] He says, "Worldliness is whatever any culture does to make sin seem normal righteousness to be strange." The culture we create shapes the landscape of destiny. The prophet Jeremiah laments the idola-

---

18 *"God in the Wasteland: the Reality of Truth in a World of Fading Dreams." God in the Wasteland: the Reality of Truth in a World of Fading Dreams, by David F. Wells, W.B. Eerdmans, 1995, p. 4.*

try that Israel had embraced when he said, in Jeremiah 2:11, "Has a nation changed gods when they were not gods? But My people have changed their glory for that which does not profit."

Culture was designed to be glorious because, through it, mankind was to reflect the Glory of God. When we look at a culture or aspects of a culture that is far from being glorious, we often see a hopeless emptiness. The people have become like the empty darkened gods they serve. How do people end up in this condition? Through the prophet Jeremiah, God describes how even the righteous can drift into emptiness.

"And walked after emptiness and became empty?" (Jeremiah 2:5b)

"And walked after things that did not profit." (Jeremiah 2:8b)

What you walk towards you will eventually reach. The hope given mankind through Jesus Christ is that through encountering conviction, you can change direction. You can repent, turn around, walk in another direction and seek the Lord. Your beliefs are flexible, and by default, the culture your beliefs create can be altered. The world around you can begin to look like the heaven inside you.

Flexibility is one of the beautiful aspects of how God designed the system of culture. It is like a living work of art constantly being shaped and molded by supernatural forces that are made manifest through human assent, beliefs, and practices. Here is the challenge of culture. Culture is under constant tension between being a manifestation of the ways of God or a manifestation of the counterfeit world system that is informed by the enemy. Culture is never static because the human condition is never static. Culture was designed to be shaped, and it is always morphing in one direction or another, taking on new characteristics or emanating new definitions of "normal." The original design of this transformational process is that normal culture on earth would eventually look like the normal culture found in heaven. What mankind beholds the world becomes.

We all have an inherent ability to influence. As part of God's sovereign design he has allowed your choices to matter and your influence to last. The Lord is excited about who you are and all the potential he has given you. As a trusting father, he wants to see what you will do with all that he has provided. He delights in you and is excited to work with you to steward creation. The right response to this great trust is to be faithful influencers. Influence is how your metron will be transformed for better or worse.

Chapter 16
Metron Apostles

You ARE AN *APOSTLE* TO YOUR METRON. There are many different interpretations and understandings regarding the term apostle used in the New Testament. Each has a level of accuracy, and all are derived from legitimate study and interpretations. One of the generally agreed on aspects of an apostle is that part of their job description in the kingdom was to be a "sent one." These sent ones were given authority through Christ to serve as representatives of the Church, particularly through engaging with unchurched regions of the world.

I believe there is one especially helpful understanding of the original title "Apostle" or *Apostolos* (ἀπόστολος) when we view the word in the historical context of Jesus time on earth. Why did he choose to use the word apostle when he gave a job description to his disciples? That an apostle is a sent one is accurate, but there is more to the definition when viewed through the lens of the expansive Roman Empire at that time. To the average person in that empire, the title "apostle" would have been associated with its common use in culture. The term was often used to describe an "envoy." Consider this brief description and word study from an anonymous author.

> *"The concept of an apostle was invented by the Phoenician empire and used heavily by the Romans. When the Roman army conquered a new nation, a new culture (something they did with remarkable regularity!), the Emperor would send an Apostolos. It was the name given to the lead ship in a fleet of ships sent from Rome to the new land, and especially for the man — one man — who led that fleet. The fleet — and that man — were carrying the embodiment of Rome with them to the new territory.*

"The apostle's job description in Roman culture is functionally the foundation for the apostle's job in the Church: to bring the home civilization to the new territory. In Rome's day, the apostle brought Rome's legal system, education system, language, government, financial systems, entertainment, culture. His job was to make the new culture fit into the Roman empire, to become Roman, to the degree that when Caesar arrived, he'd feel at home in the new territory."

This understanding of what an apostle was to do helps us understand our role within a metron. Rather than attempting to establish Roman Empire culture in new lands, we establish kingdom culture in the land of our metron. It is not Caesar or a worldly entity that we are serving but the King of Kings and Lord of Lords. The physical and spiritual condition of our metron constantly ebbs and flows and requires continual cultivation if it is to become pleasant and welcoming to the presence of God.

In your God-given sphere of influence, many hostile forces are willfully bringing chaos into the ecosystem you are managing. Sin, corruption, forces of evil, sinful human wills, and the fallen condition of creation all factor into the condition of your metron. All of these factors influence the amount of "fitting in" to the kingdom that your metron can achieve. We have to reflect constantly on the promise Jesus gave us that he is greater than the world and that we are able to overcome because of his greatness in us.

"You are from God, little children, and have overcome them; because greater is he who is in you than he who is in the world." (1 John 4:4)

Often when managing a metron, even when we seem to do everything right, things turn out wrong. This seems to be the case when looking at the world around us and even within our metron. Frustration and disillusionment often occur if we don't first attend to the spiritual connections in our garden. If we don't manage the spiritual factors first, then, often, the physical or natural aspects in our metron never come into proper alignment with the culture of heaven. This reality is an outworking of God's original design. In the kingdom, God designed that the *outside* would look like the *inside*. What is visible would be a reflection of what is invisible. While the inside and outside conditions of your metron are spiritual and important, there is an order of events indicated by Jesus.

"You blind Pharisee, first clean the inside of the cup and of the dish, so that the outside of it may become clean also." (Matthew 23:26)

Where does the "cleaning" or "work" begin in this statement? Jesus emphasizes that the internal comes first, and once that is "cleaned" then the external will come into alignment.

If heaven is truly within you, then there is nothing that can stop you from "heavenizing" that which is around you. Don't be frustrated when you can't seem to make progress in the external aspect of your metron. Use the frustration and concern you feel to look inside the cup and see what you should do to become more like Christ. You can't get everyone into heaven, but you can get heaven into everyone who you influence. Remember, it starts with your relationship with God. You need to first cultivate the right culture of relationship and worship with your heavenly father before you try to cultivate that in the world around you.

Remember, you are truly a cultural apostle, and God has sent you into a metron as an envoy for the culture of heaven. If you are successful at fulfilling the original commission, you will bring the home civilization to the new, but very needy, territory. Once people experience the kingdom, they want to meet the King.

Evaluate the internal condition of your metron each day and ask this question, "Lord, do you feel welcome and comfortable when we are abiding together in the garden you have given me?" Your commission and privilege is to manage your metron in such a way that when Jesus arrives in your garden, he feels like he is right at home. All of a sudden, you might realize that things are on earth as they are in heaven.

Designed and Assigned

God has designed and assigned a perfect metron for you. Your garden needs you because it needs the presence of God. You are a conduit through which the presence of God arrives.

In the beginning, God's design was that the created order would be "on earth as it is in heaven." Whatever else heaven may be, it is an environment where father God will gather his children to himself, and humanity will abide with their creator. In the discussion regarding what was actually going on in the Garden of Eden, the original design was relationship. The model of unhindered relationship between creator and creation was at the heart of God's plan. The original commission that gave purpose and guidance to humanity was established on the premise that they would live in perfect harmony with God and cultivate an atmosphere of worship within their environment. This atmosphere of right relationship and worship is what Adam was to cultivate not only in the garden but in the areas of creation that were yet to be subdued. Worship is the response of connection the divine and the evidence of right relationship between created and creator.

The garden was the initial connection point between heaven and earth. This was where the kingdom of heaven flowed down, and all creation looked up. This is where we see that a culture of unbroken relationship with his people was God's original design. This was the original temple, or "Garden Temple" as theologian G.K. Beal discusses in his brilliant book *The Temple and the Church's Mission*.

"That the garden of Eden was the first sacred space is also suggested by observing that Solomon's temple was described with botanical and arboreal imagery that gave it a garden-like appearance." (G.K. Beale)[19]

What was happening in the garden gave a point of reference that informed a recurring narrative throughout scripture and would culminate in the ultimate victory at the Cross of Christ. As we explore these defining moments in spiritual history, we will realize new depths and dimensions of the victory that Christ won. His death and resurrection reaffirmed God's original design and empowered us ultimately to fulfill the original commission.

"Once, on being asked by the Pharisees when the Kingdom of God would come, Jesus replied, 'The coming of the Kingdom of God is not something that can be observed, nor will people say, "Here it is," or, "There it is," because the Kingdom of God is in your midst [within you].'" (Luke 17:20–21)

Adam was cultivating the connection between the garden and heaven through stewarding the presence of God. Today, the kingdom influencer serves as a conduit for heaven to touch earth. The presence of God and all

---

19 *G.K. Beale, The Temple and the Church's Mission, page 71*

that originates in him is intended to flow through you to the world around you. Jesus makes it clear that the Kingdom of God is within you, and it influences the reality that is around you.

Chapter 17
Commissioned and Recommissioned

GOD IS NOT ONLY HIGHLY INVESTED IN the original design for creation but is also persistent about implementation. Scripture gives an account of the commissioning and recommissioning of God's influencers in the course of history. There are several history makers found throughout the scriptural and historical time line that are helpful to review. When we don't know where we came from, it's hard to know where we are. Where we have ended up in the course of spiritual history is a brilliant fulfillment of God's original plans and purposes.

To better understand how you ended up with this job of managing a metron, we need to start back at the beginning.

We recall that in the Garden of Eden, God gave Adam and Eve the original commission. After mankind sins and creation is cursed, God launches a plan of redemption that would span from Adam all the way to you.

"God blessed them; and God said to them, 'Be fruitful and multiply, and fill the earth, and subdue it; and rule over the fish of the sea and over the birds of the sky and over every living thing that moves on the earth.'" (Genesis 1:28)

The command continues from Adam onward; "Spread out, fill the earth and subdue it." God has always been committed to connecting with his creation and he has always chosen to do it through mankind. Though Adam and Eve initially failed to fulfill the original commission, God maintained his purposes by expelling them from the garden. Apparently, they had not yet left the garden to complete their commission. Even though when they were removed from the garden, this set them on a redemptive course to cultivate creation. In a manner that only God could orchestrate, we see that what is easily perceived as punishment turned out to be a path to obedience. In the kingdom, God's discipline in our lives is intended to lead us into our destiny.

Noah

Noah received the same original commission given to Adam. In Genesis 9, we see that God's original design and the mandate he gave to Adam is restated to Noah after the flood. God says in Genesis 9:1, "And God blessed Noah and his sons and said to them, "Be fruitful and multiply, and fill the earth."

In Genesis 9:7, the Lord reiterates this command saying, "As for you, be fruitful and multiply; Populate the earth abundantly and multiply in it." One translation of this verse reads as "swarm in the earth!"

The Lord makes his point again in Genesis 9:8 by clearly telling Noah and his family that he is reestablishing his original covenant with mankind. Verses 8 and 9 say, "Then God spoke to Noah and to his sons with him, saying, 'Now behold, I Myself do establish My covenant with you, and with your descendants after you.'"

God is making it very clear that his original mandate and design still stand. Through Noah and his family God intended that mankind would multiply, spread out, and subdue the earth.

Tower of Babel

After Noah, we come to the Tower of Babel. Again we see that mankind is well aware of God's mandate to spread out and fill the earth, but they are rebelling and rejecting the commission that was given to Noah. Similar to Adam, they did not want to leave their garden to fill the earth and subdue it. So God intervened again and disciplined them so they could reach their destiny.

"Now the whole world had one language and a common speech. As people moved eastward, they found a plain in Shinar and settled there. They said to each other, 'Come, let's make bricks and bake them thoroughly.' They used brick instead of

stone, and tar for mortar. Then they said, 'Come, let us build ourselves a city, with a tower that reaches to the heavens, so that we may make a name for ourselves; otherwise we will be scattered over the face of the whole earth.'" (Genesis 11:1–4)

One deeper lesson illustrated in the story of Babel is that the nature of man, the intent (or inclination) of man's heart is evil from his youth. See Genesis 8:21. In our nature is the deep awareness that we were created in the likeness of God and that our true identity is found in the presence of our Father in whose likeness we were created. The sin of the people of Babel is much like the sin of Satan. Isaiah 14:13–14, quotes Satan as saying, "But you said in your heart, 'I will ascend to heaven; I will raise my throne above the stars of God, And I will sit on the mount of assembly In the recesses of the north. I will ascend above the heights of the clouds; I will make myself like the Most High.'"

It was Satan who said, "I will ascend to Heaven." With whom do you think the people of Babel were aligning? God's covenant, mandate, and command were that mankind "spread out, fill the earth and subdue it." Satan's goal was to reach upwards and attempt to subdue heaven and make himself like the "Most High." So the people of Babel aligned with the vain designs of God's enemy and tried to ascend into heaven via a giant tower. In their rebellion and self will they imagined that they would be able to do things their way. Their aim became staying together in the land of Shinar and avoiding God's original design to spread out and fill the earth.

Both Satan and the people of Babel wanted to get to heaven on their terms and in their strength. They wanted to do things their way in God's universe. This was an undertaking born of rebellion and self-will. The people of Babel said we need to reach heaven on our own and make a name for ourselves so that we will "not be scattered over the face of the earth."

Not only was the rebellion at Babel aligned with Satan's goals but it illustrated a completely wrong understanding of God's original design for how he chooses to connect with man. In the Garden of Eden, God showed himself to be the "God who comes down." He would come down and meet with Adam. Again we see in this scenario at Babel God showing himself to be the God who comes down and meets with man.

"But the Lord came down to see the city and the tower the people were building. The Lord said, "If as one people speaking the same language they have begun to

do this, then nothing they plan to do will be impossible for them. Come, let us go down and confuse their language so they will not understand each other." So the Lord scattered them from there over all the earth, and they stopped building the city. That is why it was called Babel—because there the Lord confused the language of the whole world. From there the Lord scattered them over the face of the whole earth." (Genesis 11:5—9)

Second Chances

An interesting side note to the original commission is the recurring emphasis on being "scattered over the face of the earth." The word scattered conjures up a mental image of a farmer throwing out handfuls of seed into his field. The idea of forcible coercion and dispersion seems to be carried by the word "scattered." In the context of God's redemptive original design for mankind, the initiative was put on Adam to "spread out" and "fill the earth." It was given to mankind to obey, but when they continued to resist and rebel, they were scattered and forced to fill the earth.

God will ultimately accomplish his will, but the willing partnership and cooperation of mankind are often seen in scripture to be a variable. If mankind had willingly obeyed and partnered with God to spread out and fill the earth and subdue it, would there have been the scattering and confusion of the languages at Babel? The obedient option would bring blessing while the correction was accomplished through discipline. Mankind chose the corrective option by their rebellion. From this pivotal moment in spiritual history, we see the emergence of what are technically known as "ethnolinguistic people groups" or ethnic groups. Although before the dispersion at Babel, there are a few references to other distinct ethnolinguistic groups, it seems it was not the norm. The scripture clearly states in Genesis 11:6 "... as one people speaking the same language." The general condition of mankind was defined by a unified identity and language. Scripture also indicates that they were also unified in their rebellion against God.

Merciful Misery

The Lord disciplines us so that we can reach our destiny. Languages and ethnic groups were formed out of this collective discipline at Babel. God was not only intent on mankind fulfilling his original commission to spread out and fill the earth, but he also had the goal of blessing and reconciling in mind. The scattering that God enacted at Babel appears to be a form of punishment at first read, but it actually is redemptive in its ultimate purpose. We see this in the writings of the Apostle Paul.

In Acts 17:26–27 Paul said, while preaching on Mars Hill in Athens, "He made from one man every nation of mankind to live on all the face of the earth, having determined their appointed times and the boundaries of their habitation, that they would seek God, if perhaps they might grope for him and find him, though he is not far from each one of us."

Paul graciously expressed the redemptive purposes of God as he spoke with the people of Athens about their original design and the purposes of God. The first redemptive outcome articulated in this dialogue is that God ultimately made man to "live on all the face of the earth." To spread out and fill the earth. The second redemptive purpose behind the dispersion of the nations or *ethne*, was that they would have the chance, the opportunity genuinely to seek out reconciliation and relationship with their creator.

In the Babel story, God observes that if they continue as "one people and the same language," mankind would become united in rebellion and self will against the Lord. By diversifying and dispersing them to fill the earth, he actually short-circuited their united rebellion and saved them from judgment. What might appear to be a form of judgment actually became merciful discipline. He enacted the ancient strategy of "divide and conquer." Not in a military sense but with the goal of conquering mankind's heart through love. By the divine wisdom of his discipline, the Lord made mankind inherently miserable and desperate by breaking them up into nations.

The purpose of this discipline was that they would be so miserable that "they would seek God" and that they would be given the motivation to "grope for him and find him." The aim of the Lord is always the restoration of a relationship with man. Through the formation and dispersion of the *ethne* or nations, God positioned man in the best possible way for reconciliation with him.

In Babel, God finds mankind aligning with the author of rebellion, Satan. Just like their new "god," mankind is working to try to create their own redemption. They are trying to ascend to heaven by their own means. Satan always wants to ascend; God always humbles himself and comes down. Tragically, when mankind aligns with the world system, we see a constant attempt through our own efforts to "become like the most high." We, like the people of Babel, try to reach heaven on our terms, and create our own salvation. Ultimately, this is the deception that every false religion is built upon. Every manifestation of the kingdom of darkness requires man to "do" something or pay a "cost" to save themselves or to create their own identity. Even humanism, the preferred religion of the developed world, requires you to attain redemption through the human effort of becoming your own god. Every demonic god that is at the heart of every false religion institutes a system that requires human effort and exacts a human cost.

There is a real sense of eternity hard-wired into every person. Every human heart longs for meaning, absolution, holiness, peace, hope, heaven, purpose, and belonging. The systems of Satan always exact a price and demand worship. The true God always pays your price and comes down to invite you up. When we truly encounter him we want to give him everything. He invites you into a beautiful relationship that answers all the needs and questions in the heart of mankind. The enemy says, "Do this, sacrifice that, offer those, climb this temple, then maybe I'll do for you…" The demands of darkness result in a yoke of slavery, but the free gift of Christ sets the captive free.

Jesus humbled himself and became a man. He set aside his divinity in order to reclaim the keys (authority and access) over all of creation. He came as the second Adam to redeem what the first Adam had lost.

Jesus prayed saying, "Your kingdom come; your will be done, on earth as it is in heaven." The focus and purpose that should now define us is the fulfillment of the Lord's prayer. If we are effective at getting his kingdom and his will expressed on earth, then the divinely ordered result will be that people will go to heaven. Inherent in the Lord's Prayer is the nature of God's engagement with mankind. He comes down so that we can go up.

Jesus came down so that we could go up. In John 6:51, Jesus says, "I am the living bread that *came down* out of heaven; if anyone eats of this bread, he will live forever…" (emphasis added)

In Psalm 18:6–9, we see how the Lord responds when King David cries out to the Lord in his time of distress.

"In my distress I called upon the Lord,
And cried to my God for help;
He heard my voice out of his temple,
And my cry for help before him came into his ears.
Then the earth shook and quaked;
And the foundations of the mountains were trembling
And were shaken, because he was angry.
Smoke went up out of his nostrils,
And fire from his mouth devoured;
Coals were kindled by it.
He bowed the heavens also and came down."

When David cried out to the Lord, God "bent the heavens…" He is the God who comes down! Strength manifested through humility is the nature of the Kingdom of God. Meekness is defined in this kingdom as "Strength under control." In the Kingdom of God, the strong serve the weak, in the kingdom of this world (and every false religion) the weak serve the strong.

While we want the King to feel comfortable when he visits our metron, the reality of our fallen world is that you cannot control all the choices and factors that affect the condition of your metron, but you can influence them. You can "own" your metron as the spiritual gatekeeper or watchman. The culture that operates in your metron is spiritually originated and spiritually sustained. The authority that is delegated to you enables you to co-author the spiritual operating system that functions in your metron. If you manage your metron spiritually, much of the outward or natural chaos of your world will be subdued around you. This understanding enables you to operate as a ruler and servant. Managing your metron requires you to rule spiritually and serve naturally.

Reconnecting

Many generations after Noah and the great dispersion at the tower of Babel, God chooses a Kushite descendant of Noah to become the next connection point between Heaven and Earth. Abram was an elderly man who

God chose to be the "father of many nations" as Scripture states. Through the course of Abram's relationship with God, he receives a new name, Abraham, and he receives a recommissioning. God commands Abraham to move out and bring blessing to all the people groups on earth.

Genesis 12:1–3 says, "The Lord had said to Abram, "Go from your country, your people and your father's household to the land I will show you. I will make you into a great nation, and I will bless you; I will make your name great, and you will be a blessing. I will bless those who bless you, and whoever curses you I will curse; and all peoples on earth will be blessed through you." (NIV)

The Heart of the Original Commission

This is God revealing his deeper purpose for the original commission. God intends to reconnect with his creation and to do this he promises Abraham that all nations will be blessed through him. The purpose of the original commission is reaffirmed as *connection*. Connection between heaven and earth, through the connection point of a man named Abraham. Abraham became a new one-person garden through whom God would advance the footprint of heaven into the dark corners of the earth. God promised Abraham that he would produce a "garden nation"—Israel. Abraham and his offspring nation carried the same original commission to multiply, fill the earth, and subdue it.

Spreading out and subduing through cultivation, i.e., Work, Worship, and Connection were intended to bring blessing to all aspects of creation. What was the blessing prophesied to Abraham? He is told that "through you, all nations will be blessed." Through Abraham's line Jesus Christ would come, and the blessing of personal salvation would be made available to all who would repent and embrace his kingdom. The apostle Paul revisits the commission God gave to Abraham and clarifies what exactly the "blessing" is that would come through him.

"The Scripture foresaw that God would justify the Gentiles by faith, and announced the Gospel in advance to Abraham: [saying]... 'All nations will be blessed through you.'" (Galatians 3:8)

God came down to Abraham to begin the reconnection process with mankind. The gospel or "good news" was the promise of God's design for reconciliation, forgiveness, and restoration. Much Old Testament scripture points towards the coming of the Messiah, the savior, and coming king. The prophet Isaiah reaffirms the good news of blessing and the nature of the coming Kingdom of God when he prophesied in Isaiah 9:6–7 saying, "For a child will be born to us, a son will be given to us; And the government will rest on his shoulders; And his name will be called Wonderful Counselor, Mighty God, Eternal Father, Prince of Peace. There will be no end to the increase of his government or of peace."

The connection that God made through his relationship and promises to Abraham are then manifest in the nation of Israel. Israel descends from Abraham, and they carry the same commission that Abraham received. Temples and tabernacles become the new conduit through which the presence of God connects from heaven to earth. Israel emerges as the new garden. They were blessed with the presence of God and carried the commission to spread that blessing to all nations.

Remember, the blessing that God promised to Abraham is the restoration of connection and relationship between God and man. In scripture, God's relationship with Israel is often demonstrated by a tabernacle or temple that is intriguingly similar to the garden that it was emulating in its design. God chose to establish the tabernacles and temples in Israel as the place where his glory would dwell.

Just as the Garden of Eden was a central connection point of relationship with God, the tabernacles and temples had a central and "protected" place of connection. The innermost chamber was called the "holy of holies." Outside this was the "holy place" and beyond the holy place were the "outer courts" or the "court of the Gentiles." Through this recurring construction blueprint, God points us back towards the beginning original design. The Garden and the temples carried a distinct footprint of heaven that point us toward the current realities of the kingdom on earth.

Chapter 18

The Footprint of Heaven

"The Lord God planted a garden toward the east, in Eden; and there he placed the man whom he had formed." (Genesis 2:8)

THERE WAS A THREE-PART MODEL CLEARLY PORTRAYED in the original design of creation; earth, Eden, and the garden. Later in scripture, we see that the garden becomes the template for Israel's temples. Both the garden and the temples that followed were designed as places where heaven and earth would meet.

The temples and various tabernacle venues that we see in Israel's history served as footprints of heaven on the landscape of earth. In the account of the construction of the first temple in Israel there are fascinating descriptions that align the temple with its roots in the Garden of Eden. 1st Kings 6:32, "And on the two olive-wood doors he carved cherubim, palm trees, and open flowers, and overlaid the cherubim and palm trees with hammered gold."

There are frequent references in the carving to cherubim, palm trees, flowers and copious amounts of gold and jewels. All of these elements were mentioned in Genesis as being in and around the garden and in Eden.

1st Kings 7:42 describes that pomegranates were a highlight of garden history. They were prominently featured as decorations in the temple!

No physical temple can "contain" God, but part of his original design is to establish connection points with his people through which he would cooperatively manage creation. The connection always starts with planting a garden—contained environment of order and relationship with his creation. One would think that since God is omnipresent, he wouldn't have any use for a particular connection point in the natural realm. But humans need a reference point. Whether that is the north star for navigation or a garden as a point of reference, we need help not only getting around geo-graphically, but we also need help finding God.

God makes himself readily available to the one who would seek for him. God has used these defined connection points to make himself accessible and to create a contrast between the place his glory dwells and the fallen world around us. The contrast between the condition of the cultivated Garden of Eden with its unbroken atmosphere of worship and perfectly managed creation and the world outside the garden must have been nota-ble. One was beautifully ordered, and the other was not. One was sub-dued through cultivation, and the other was not. One contained mankind, and the other was waiting on Adam's offspring to multiply and fill the earth. Similarly, the condition of the holy of holies inside the tabernacles and temples was distinct from the outside world. In these geographically specific connection points, there was a "garden" so to speak in which God's glory chose to dwell and interact with mankind.

There is an intriguing correlation found in scripture regarding God's manifest presence in the temple and the presence of God in the garden. This correlation is commented on by theologian G.K. Beal. He writes, "Israel's temple was the place where the priest experienced God's unique presence, and Eden was the place where Adam walked and talked with God. The same Hebrew verbal form *mithallek* used for God's "walking back and forth" in the garden (Gen. 3:8), also describes God's presence in the tabernacle (Lev. 26:12; Deuteronomy 23:14 [15]; 2 Sam. 7:6–7)."[20]

In the kingdom, points of connection always start in a garden but are never intended to be contained. The very nature of the Kingdom of God is that it is advancing and moving forward. Expansion is the key intention found in the original design of the garden, the temples and is now also seen in you and me. Adam was commissioned to expand and fill the earth, Noah was commissioned to expand and fill the earth, Israel was likewise commissioned to expand and use their Abrahamic blessing to be a blessing to all creation. Now you and I have inherited the original commission. God has now made his presence mobile. He still has chosen to connect with creation through a garden, but now that garden is inside of you.

At the resurrection of Christ, things get really exciting. The presence of God was no longer geographically located nor contained in a physical

---

20 G.K. Beale, *The Temple and the Church's Mission* p.66

garden or buildings made with human hands. Under the New Covenant you, the spiritual descendant of Abraham are the new garden. You who are of faith in Christ are his new temple, yet you carry an old commission. Jesus' death overcame the separation sin had created between God and his children. The broken relationship between God and mankind was violently removed, and the connection was re-established.

> *"And when Jesus had cried out again in a loud voice, he gave up his spirit. At that moment the curtain of the temple was torn in two from top to bottom. The earth shook, the rocks split..."*(Matthew 27:50–51 NIV)

When Jesus "gave up his spirit," the curtain that separated the holy of holies from the rest of creation was torn from top to bottom; God was on the move. He still utilized his original design as the God who comes down, connects, occupies, and spreads out. This time the nature of his abode was completely different; he made his home in you, and you are mobile.

Mobile Temples

At the cross, everything changed, and still, the garden model remained. Through the death and resurrection of Jesus, God established the ultimate and permanent connection point between heaven and earth. In the Kingdom of God, a new dynamic was begun. Soon, millions of mobile garden temples will have been created through faith in Christ. Heaven's connection point to earth was fully established. This myriad of mobile connection points became an unstoppable conduit through which the Kingdom of God, the very presence of God, gushed like rivers of living water.

> *"He who believes in Me, as the Scripture said, 'From his innermost being will flow rivers of living water.'"*(John 7:38)

Four rivers flowed out from the original Garden of Eden to water the earth. Now rivers of living water flow out of your innermost being (John 7:38.) The kingdom is within you, but God intends that everything would be cultivated and subdued into the domain of the king. In God's design, we find that what is inside of you flows out to everything around you. As a believer, you are now a pipeline of living water sourced in heaven and bringing life to creation. If rivers of living water are truly flowing from your innermost being, you cannot help but restore and revive your metron. Your metron is desperately thirsty for the water of life that flows out of you. To be confident in your calling to manage metrons you must be convinced of your identity, and that you have something to offer. What you have to offer is all that God has given you. Your position in the kingdom is secure.

> *"Do you not know that you are a temple of God and that the Spirit of God dwells in you?"* (1Cor. 3:16)

> *"Or do you not know that your body is a temple of the Holy Spirit who is in you, whom you have from God, and that you are not your own?"* (1Cor. 6:19)

You are authorized and commissioned to pull the realities of heaven into your metron. This is the true fulfillment of the prayer that Jesus taught his disciples to pray in Matthew 6:10. "Your kingdom come. Your will be done, On earth as it is in heaven." Heaven is not only a future destination, but it is a present reality since the spirit of God truly lives inside you.

When his will is being done in you, your metron will be flooded by living water. Your identity in Christ is as a living garden temple in which you co-labor with God to fulfill the original commission.

Inside this commission, you plan along these lines.

- Cultivate
- Keep
- Multiply
- Spread Out
- Fill the Earth
- Subdue

You may not consider yourself seriously interested in gardening, but when you become a follower of Christ, not only did you receive the original commission to cultivate and keep a garden but you also became a garden. All of the preceding modalities of God's original design in Biblical history have now culminated in you. More specifically, everything has been summed up in Christ as explained in Ephesians 1:10 "...with a view to an administration suitable to the fullness of the times, that is, the summing up of all things in Christ, things in the heavens and things on the earth."

Christ's Spirit now resides in you. Your very body is now the garden temple of the Holy Spirit, and the presence of God now flows from you like the rivers that flowed out of the Garden of Eden. The Garden watered the world, and now you likewise are commissioned to water your metron.

Jesus preached that the "Kingdom of God is within you." Your streams of living water originate in his kingdom. When you genuinely become a "new creature in Christ Jesus" (2 Corinthians 5:17.) Your soul explodes with life, hope, beauty, and joy... just like the Garden of Eden. When Jesus rules over you, and you spiritually impact your metron, i.e. spheres of influence, then the kingdom has truly come, and the righteous reign of Jesus is enacted.

Jesus said the kingdom is within you. His spirit resides in you. The world around you begins to look like the world within you. You shape your metron by the thoughts, words, and deeds that emanate from the garden in your heart. As the culture of heaven flourishes in your heart, the ruins in your metron will experience the compassion of the Lord.

Getting Heaven into Earth

"The Lord will surely comfort Zion and will look with compassion on all her ru-ins; he will make her deserts like Eden, her wastelands like the garden of the Lord. Joy and gladness will be found in her, thanksgiving and the sound of singing." (Isaiah 51:3)

I love this section of scripture. There is hope for every person, every metron, and every nation. There is a God-given promise of recovery and restoration of all that was lost through sin. This promise gives a glimpse into the Garden of Eden's appearance and into how restoration in Christ functions. This is a reflection of the "on earth as it is in heaven" prayer. Looking at the metron of life, the designated sphere of influence, we often see the same Isaiah 51 conditions.

We see ruined souls, we see deserts in our communities, and we see wastelands in our nations. We ought to have the same response to the brokenness around us that our Father expresses in this scripture. The Lord promises to restore the ruins to the condition of the first garden. The passage gives us examples of conditions in the garden and what I believe is good news for our metrons.

"Joy and gladness" are found in the restored garden. Thanksgiving and singing are heard in the garden. This is the fruit of the Gospel. This is "thy kingdom come." When your metron is actively being restored, it will begin to thrive in the presence of God. Just as the Lord promised comfort for Zion, you carry the message of the Good News of rescue, comfort, compassion, and hope. In this is the gospel of the Kingdom. Remember that through co-laboring with God, you are actively working to reverse the effects of the fall in your metron.

Chapter 19

Metrons Matter

GOD HAS MADE ROOM FOR YOU AND genuinely intends for you to work together with him in the family business. He trusts you. That you would influence and steward your metron is his original design. The way you affect your sphere of influence is determined by what you have to give. What you have to give is only what fills your heart. If your heart is full of the presence of God, then your influence will be full of wisdom and understanding. In co-laboring with Christ to manage your metron, you impart life and blessing through your values, beliefs, spirit, and character.

One significant outcome of God allowing you to co-labor with him in managing your metron is the humiliation of the enemy and the undermining of the claims of Satan. When a follower of Christ functions as a connection point with heaven, blessing is the inevitable outcome. I believe that God loves to compare and contrast his ways with the ways of this world. One primary way God does this is by allowing the decisions of both humans and spiritual beings to be consequential. These decisions are truly significant because the consequences matter.

If you do things God's way in God's universe, you will be blessed. If you do things the enemies way, or your way, in God's universe, you will not be blessed. Consequences are not always negative. Consequences of right relationship with God are good and cultivate worship and praise for the King of Kings. Consequences for rebellion and self will always lead to death and destruction.

"There is a way which seems right to a man, But its end is the way of death."
(Proverbs 16:25)

The enemy desperately wants to prove that he is just as smart and deserving of worship and praise as God.

I suggest that the Lord is willing to allow humans and the spiritual realm to recognize the infinitely superior wisdom and knowledge that arises through right relationship with God. Consequences are the key indicators that make clear to all that the word and ways of the Lord never fail. The enemy does everything possible to avoid consequences so that his claims of equality with God can never be evaluated. He preaches a false gospel of life without consequences. This false gospel leads to license and not the liberty that comes through faith in Christ.

Jesus preaches the true Gospel of life that leads to right consequences. This is liberty. The key indicator that exposes every false belief system or worldview is that you should be able to do whatever you want. You should be free to act however you want, and to avoid any negative consequences. God ensures there are consequences in the created order for your good and his glory. Every time you do things God's way in his universe the positive consequences will remind the heavenly rulers and authorities that Jesus is in charge.

You are to impart to your metron a river of living water. This living water is God's presence and is full of the wisdom and understanding that can flood your metron and displace the works of darkness. The rivers of living water that flow from within the believer (John 7:38) wash away the designs of darkness and bring life to everything in your metron. This is how God designed you to influence and grow the kingdom. The cumulative outcome of all believers managing their metrons like Adam managed the garden is the fulfillment of Christ's prayer "your kingdom come, your will be done on earth as it is in heaven." We find true meaning in life when we allow ourselves to be spiritually full and to serve as a conduit of life, bringing living water from heaven to flood the spiritual deserts of earth.

Jesus said he came to destroy the works of the devil, and he gave us all authority to do likewise. Jesus told his disciples in Matthew 28:18, "All authority has been given to Me in heaven and on earth."

The original commission to Adam and the Great Commission are all about destroying the works of darkness and reestablishing alignment with God's original design.

The Real Culture War

"For our struggle is not against flesh and blood, but against the rulers, against the powers, against the world forces of this darkness, against the spiritual forces of wickedness in the heavenly places."(Ephesians 6:12)

When you enter the "Kingdom of God" the kingdom also enters you. When the kingdom enters you, by the very nature of the process, it displaces much of what has been allowed to define you. This process is called "displacement." When displacement happens, you have to prepare for an earthquake.

You will experience the shaking effects of "displacement" when God empowers you to rewrite the corrupted source code in your metron; evil is often violently displaced. When something is displaced in your metron, there is space created to introduce the operating system of heaven into that newly created access point.

Another way to think about "displacement" is to compare it with the parallel command to "subdue" that God gives in the original commission to Adam. If Adam had been fully obedient to this part of his original mandate, he would have "displaced" the disorder outside of Eden and subdued the culture of chaos that existed outside of his initial metron.

Our new covenant re-commissioning by God is known as the "Great Commission" and is essentially a re-affirming of Adam's original commission. Under the new covenant, the way that we subdue is that we disciple. We make "disciples of all nations." By the power of the Holy Spirit and under the commissioning authority that Jesus gave us, we are called to displace darkness.

"The Son of God appeared for this purpose, to destroy the works of the devil."(1st John 3:8b)

Jesus came to destroy the works of the devil, and we are given the power and authority to follow his example. We have the privilege of completing what Adam was initially commissioned to do. Under the new covenant, it is the hearts of men and women that are subdued and cultivated through salvation and discipleship. This displacement process is ongoing in the culture of a metron. It often disrupts the normal accepted pattern of existence to which people in that "culture" are accustomed.

Think about your personal story of encountering Christ and repenting for your sins. For most of us, when we became followers of Christ, there was often a sudden and violent change in our own life culture. Our preferences, beliefs, and behaviors were shaken and sifted as if they had been the victim of a spiritual earthquake. Left standing is that which the Lord approved. That which collapsed and fell away was that which the Lord found to be from the source code of the evil one.

Any "code" that he did not author, God will edit out. This is the process of displacement, and it is also the nature of discipleship. If you are part of the Kingdom of God, then you have to anticipate that there will be earthquakes that shake the soul and rewrite the code. According to scripture, this does happen.

> "And his voice shook the earth then, but now he has promised, saying, "YET ONCE MORE I WILL SHAKE NOT ONLY THE EARTH, BUT ALSO THE HEAVEN." This expression, "Yet once more," denotes the removing of those things which can be shaken, as of created things, so that those things which cannot be shaken may remain." (Hebrews 12:26–27)

The writer of Hebrews goes on to say in verse 28–29,

> "Therefore, since we receive a kingdom which cannot be shaken, let us show gratitude, by which we may offer to God an acceptable service with reverence and awe; for our God is a consuming fire."

Our God is a consuming fire, and he is intent on demonstrating that his kingdom cannot be shaken. It is eternal, and according to this scripture, it is yours. We are receiving it.

There is another curious section of scripture that makes it clear that one effect of seeing the "kingdom come on earth as it is in heaven" is distress, division, and pain. This scripture illustrates the effects of encountering the "consuming fire" aspect of the character and nature of God.

> "I have come to cast fire upon the earth; and how I wish it were already kindled! But I have a baptism to undergo, and how distressed I am until it is accomplished! Do you suppose that I came to grant peace on earth? I tell you, no, but rather division; for from now on five members in one household will be divided, three against two and two against three. They will be divided, father against son and son against father, mother against daughter and daughter against mother,

mother-in-law against daughter-in-law and daughter-in-law against mother-in-law." (Luke 12:49—53)

The process mentioned here is not advocating domestic disputes and family disintegration. It means that the kingdom of light and the kingdom of this world do not mix. Like oil and water introduced into the same environment, there will be separation, division, distinction, and displacement. This separating or displacing effect can be costly and painful but is evidence in and of itself that the Kingdom of God is holy and separate from the ways or culture of the world. The two kingdoms cannot and will not be synchronized or mixed. Attempts to harmonize or accommodate the world system and any of its culture will collide with the promise of shaking and purging fire.

As we are transformed in Christ and the garden or metron is transformed around us, we can only expect this section of scripture to prove true. Peace is not the absence of conflict but the presence of God. The goal is the presence of God in our metron — on earth as it is in heaven.

Jesus makes it clear that there are a painful shaking and the burning that happens when a personal or corporate culture encounters the power of God. Displacement is a transformational process. The timing of this process and historical context that Jesus is alluding to in Luke 12 is open to interpretation. But the takeaway understanding that can be helpful in our current discussion is that inherently, massive disruption happens when we and our culture encounter the Kingdom of God.

The effects of a disruptive encounter with Christ should be something we excitedly anticipate! Though there is pain in the process, the prize set before us is completely worth the cost. Our question in these transformational times should always be "What beautiful thing will God bring about through this shaking process in my life or the culture of my metron?"

As we have seen in this discussion, there is no reason to be afraid of cultural transformation! It is inherent to the establishment of the kingdom. It is the mandate of every child of God to shape the culture within your metron. You are God's agents of transformation, and you have been commissioned as a cultural apostle. Your job is to align with the mandate of the original commission and cultivate the presence of God into your metron. The world around you will look like the world inside you. If you are truly a disciple of Christ, then that is "Good News" or "Gospel" for any metron because "from you will flow rivers of living water." No matter how small or how large your sphere of influence, they all want to hear the same "Gospel" or "Good News" that Jesus shared with the Samaritan woman at the well.

"Jesus answered and said to her, 'Everyone who drinks of this water will thirst again; but whoever drinks of the water that I will give him shall never thirst; but the water that I will give him will become in him a well of water springing up to eternal life.'" (John 4:13–14)

All the thirsty want the "living water" to satisfy their soul's thirst. Jesus was drawing a distinct comparison between water that quenches only the natural thirst and the *water* that Christ provides — the water that fulfills the longing of the human soul.

When the rivers of living water flow from within you, the result is that everything around you will flourish. God's original design is that you would be transformed and that the world around you would begin to look like the world inside you. Your garden or metron will thrive and grow as the living water inside you brings life to all that is around you. Not only does this flow of living water bring life, it also serves to wash away the pollution brought by sin and the enemy. The living water flowing from within you will displace the works of darkness. Your metron should glow with sanctification and life as streams of living water scour and reshape the culture within.

I exhort you, the metron manager, to consider the hope set before you and strengthen yourself in the Lord. I believe the following statements are truths of hope.

- If there is hope within you, there is hope for the nations
- If there is peace within you, there is calm for every conflict
- If there is wisdom from above within you, there is a solution for every problem
- If there is grace within you, there is restoration for every soul
- If there is light within you, there is guidance for the lost
- If the kingdom is within you, then earth can be as it is in heaven

The Ways of the Kingdom

What does it look like to influence your metron with the culture of the kingdom? Kingdom influence is the manifestation of God's ways through his word, your thoughts, and your actions. You were designed to influence and shape what you touch. This is why the world around you looks like the world inside you.

What are some of his ways? Wisdom, discernment, and understanding all overflow from the abundance of his righteousness. His ways are right. His character and nature are the very definition of right and true. Any other set of ways that are not in alignment with the character and nature of God are by definition, antichrist or the manifestation of rebellion against God.

Remember that "ways" and "culture" are the same, and both realities emanate from a spiritual root. Ways or culture are the software that is co-authored by mankind and whichever spiritual authority with which they align — aligning either with the one true God or with the "lesser" gods of this world. There are two kingdoms actively competing for your participation.

"…in which you used to live when you followed the ways of this world and of the ruler of the kingdom of the air, the spirit who is now at work in those who are disobedient." (Ephesians 2:2 NIV)

Paul mentions in his letter to the Ephesians a "kingdom of the air" that operates on the software called "ways of this world." This kingdom is where we all used to live. In contrast, we now live in the Kingdom of God as the Apostle indicates in these two scriptures.

"…and raised us up with him, and seated us with him in heavenly places in Christ Jesus." (Ephesians 2:6)

When we become followers of Christ, we are stationed in our eternal position with Christ even while we live out our commissioned life on earth. As believers, our new reality is that we manage our metron from a place of authority and a position of influence. We positively influence because we have access to the presence of God. The culture of heaven is now able to flow unhindered through you into your metron on earth. You have become the conduit of blessing that is connected to the source of life.

"For he rescued us from the domain [literally: authority] of darkness, and trans-ferred us to the kingdom of his beloved Son."(Col 1:13)

When you submitted to the lordship of Christ, your spirit immediately was relocated. You likely did not move geographically when you became a Christian, but the geography within your metron fell under a new juris-diction. There is more to come of the Kingdom of God as the spiritual trajectory of history unfolds, but right now, you are no longer a victim of darkness but a viceroy from heaven.

You are living in the Kingdom of God right now, and the Kingdom of God is living in you. Until Christ's return, there is a fully functioning domain of darkness, a "kingdom of the air" that is at work through disobe-dience. All thoughts and actions serve to either reinforce the Kingdom of God or the kingdom of the air. Culture is being crafted in your metron, and the "ways" that form its operating system will come from the kingdom to which it is connected.

Deciding who's ways will rule in your sphere of influence is the fun-damental job description of every believer. Establishing the kingdom is a matter of stewarding a pipeline or a watercourse filled with the presence of God into your sphere of influence.

Chapter 20

Navigating your Commission

IF WE ARE TO UNDERSTAND OUR PURPOSE, we have to embrace our identity as the *co-missioned*.

Commissioned: the act of committing or entrusting a person, group, etc., with supervisory power or authority.

We are entrusted with supervisory power and authority by our heavenly father to influence his creation and carry out his purposes. We are not alone in this, but we are coworkers with Christ. We are on a mission together with our Lord and savior, thus the term co-missioned. Co-(together) Mission (a sending or being sent for some duty or purpose.)

Embracing the reality that as sons and daughters of the King and brothers and sisters of Christ, requires that we embrace our role as influencers. Influence runs in the family you could say. The nature of influence, as defined in the dictionary, is "the capacity to affect the character, development, or behavior of someone or something, or the effect itself." Influence is the ability to affect. *Affect* is defined as "causing something or bringing it about." If we look one level deeper, we realize that influence, itself, is morally neutral as a "capacity" or "mechanism." It is the nature of influence that it is informed or empowered by something or someone. Influence is a mechanism for co-creation to be used by the co-missioned. God included this in his original design for creation. What matters is the type of "affect" an influencer will have in their metron. What are you going to "cause" or "bring about?"

Life often seems to be frustrating and without fulfillment, for which we then blame God. Such disillusionment is often directly related to the drifting and dissipating lifestyle we live due to lack of purpose. It is easy to become so focused on what can only be seen dimly through the telescope of our academic theological constructs that the beauty inches away is missed. Purpose and meaning are right at your fingertips. Deep inside, we know that we were created with the drive to build, improve, and accomplish. The awareness that we have a metron is deeply seated in our original design, and all of mankind has an inner compulsion to shape the world around them.

Frustration sets in if we find ourselves unable to make a difference in the world. We struggle to walk in wisdom and understanding in the fallen and broken world around us. Our quest for purpose and meaning, even as Christians, often seems to be dark and confusing. We put one foot in front of the other, hoping that things will simply work out, embracing a Christian form of fatalism. This is more closely aligned with the Islamic view of life than the Kingdom of God. Islam says, "*Inshallah*" or, "If God wills it…" Christians often similarly say, "If it's God's will."

For a Christian, this statement is not an expression of surrender to circumstances and abdication of personal responsibility. It is a way of stating interdependence and deference to our creator. It is a humbling of one's self before God. We are co-laborers with Christ Jesus. In our co-laboring we find purpose, but not by saying *inshallah*. We ask the Lord, "What should we do?" Together with our loving Father we seek to shape our garden, to cultivate it into alignment with his kingdom.

As the Ways of God transform the inner-being, we are privileged to radiate the presence of God like rivers of living water into our metron. The living water is the power of the Holy Spirit flowing through you to bring life to a dry and weary land. To realize the transformational potential of the Gospel, we must stand in a place of vision, hope and active partnership with God. In this mode of co-laboring, we can see his kingdom come, and his will be done, on earth as it is in heaven.

By taking responsibility for our metron and co-laboring with Christ, we have nothing to lose and everything to gain. If we are to err in life, then it is better to err on the side of being a responsible servant who is found exceedingly faithful with his Father's belongings and interests. Being found by the master to be a self-centered, lazy steward is an error from which you do not recover.

If you are truly fulfilling your role in the original commission, your metron should increasingly glow with the presence of God. This glow is the presence of God inside of you that must not be hidden.

"You are the light of the world. A city set on a hill cannot be hidden; nor does anyone light a lamp and put it under a basket, but on the lampstand, and it gives light to all who are in the house. Let your light shine before men in such a way that they may see your good works, and glorify your Father who is in heaven." (Matthew 5:14–16)

Everyone in your "house" needs light. Jesus said that you are to give that light to mankind so they will ultimately glorify God. You are the light of the world, a city on a hill, a cultivator of good works that testify to the hope of heaven.

You have been designed and positioned to displace darkness and replace it with the light of God. The world around you begins to look like the world inside you, and just like your heavenly Father, your words carry power. The first practical way that your light shines is through the very words that come out of your mouth. Your words carry power and authority. God spoke the world into being, and like your Father, you have the delegated authority to build up or tear down with your words.

"Death and life are in the power of the tongue, And those who love it will eat its fruit." (Proverbs 18:21)

Whatever is in abundance in the heart will ultimately shape one's metron and that shaping generally starts with words.

"The good man out of the good treasure of his heart brings forth what is good; and the evil man out of the evil treasure brings forth what is evil; for his mouth speaks from that which fills his heart." (Luke 6:45)

For better or worse, like Adam, you will influence your metron. Whether you want to or not, you are a world shaper, and like Adam, no one gets out of here without naming some animals. Are there animals that need names in your metron? What defines your life and what matters to God is how you manage your metron and co-labor toward the restoration of all things. Your sphere of responsibility is right here and right now. Whatever environment you influence is where you are to be found faithful and fruitful. There are several valid perspectives and interpretations of scripture regarding the beginning and the end of all things. But Jesus seems to make one thing clear in scripture—we are to be faithful stewards between the past and the future that will unfold.

"Be dressed ready for service and keep your lamps burning, like servants waiting for their master to return from a wedding banquet, so that when he comes and knocks they can immediately open the door for him. It will be good for those servants whose master finds them watching when he comes. Truly I tell you, he will dress himself to serve, will have them recline at the table and will come and wait on them. It will be good for those servants whose master finds them ready, even if he comes in the middle of the night or toward daybreak."(Luke 12:35—38 NIV)

I once heard it said that "the only end times you should be concerned about are your own end times." Our own "end times" will find us being held accountable in the way the watchful and ready servants are in Luke 12:39—40. "But understand this: If the owner of the house had known at what hour the thief was coming, he would not have let his house be broken into. You also must be ready, because the Son of Man will come at an hour when you do not expect him."

The parable of the watchful servants is helpful for us as we navigate our way through life in our metron.

"But about that day or hour no one knows, not even the angels in heaven, nor the Son, but only the Father."(Matthew 24:36 NIV)

Once we understand God's original design, we will find incredible joy in the journey. If we can get free from preoccupation with the "day or hour" which the scripture clearly says no one knows, we can be free to be about our Father's business.

"And he said to them, 'Why is it that you were looking for Me? Did you not know that I had to be in My Father's house?'"(Luke 2:49)

Literally, "in my father's house" means "about my father's affairs" or "the things of my father." Like Jesus, as his "brothers and sisters" we too should be "about our father's affairs."

You are called and equipped to manage whatever metron your father sees fit to delegate to you.

Chapter 21
Coding your Metron

CONSIDER WHAT IS WRITTEN IN EPHESIANS 3:10, "His intent was that now, through the church, the manifold wisdom of God should be made known to the rulers and authorities in the heavenly realms."

The dictionary defines manifold simply as "many and various." The word also carries the meaning of "multi-colored" or "multi-faceted." The manifold wisdom of God is the many and various facets of the "all knowing-ness" of God. The manifold wisdom of God is made available to you through your relationship with God and your understanding of the word of God. There is nothing in your metron that you will not be able to manage when you follow the paths of God's wisdom toward heavenly solutions.

One of the key roles of the church is to beautifully undermine the claims of darkness. This undermining of deception comes through the manifold wisdom of God that will be made known through the "Church." This mandate applies to every believer, all who are part of the Church. This commission might seem abstract and far removed from a believer's daily life experience, but it is not. As with all things that the Lord designed, there is guidance to be found in the scripture.

How does the mandate to the church in Ephesians 3:10 happen practically? How is the manifold wisdom of God to be made known through God's people? The wisdom of God is the source code of heaven. The software of blessing that God created to order his creation. Isaiah the prophet painted a picture of the process by which God co-labors with his people to bring the source code of heaven to bless the metrons of the earth.

The Source Code

"And many peoples will come and say, 'Come, let us go up to the mountain of the Lord, to the house of the God of Jacob; that he may teach us concerning his ways And that we may walk in his paths.'" (Isaiah 2:3)

Here we find a simple model of co-laboring and cooperation that shapes the world around us. Three distinct elements stand out in this model.

1. "go up." The vital first step is that we approach the Lord. "Let us then approach God's throne of grace with confidence..." (Hebrews 4:16) Through the work of Christ, we can boldly and confidently approach the Lord.
2. "that he may teach us concerning his ways." This next step is where things get really exciting. At the throne or in the presence of God, we are taught by the Lord about his ways. The manifold wisdom of God is accessible to us, redeemed children of the King. The learning of his "ways" is the natural outcome of abiding in God. This is the realm of personal relationship with God. This is where study of the word and active participation with the Holy Spirit begin to inform your every thought and action. You begin to truly be transformed by the renewing of your mind, as the Bible says.
3. "that we may walk in his paths." Once we sit at his feet and learn the ways of the Lord, we realize we are to cultivate in our garden. We become like what we behold, and as we abide in the Lord, we learn his ways. The world around us looks like the world within us, and our garden or metron begins to look like heaven.

The heaven that each believer lives daily in the presence of the Lord is then manifest into each person's sphere of influence. Suddenly, you may find yourself "walking in the cool of day" (Gen 3:8) alongside the Lord. Now your metron on earth is cultivated as a model of the kingdom, and the presence of God begins to expand the atmosphere of heaven into the ends of the earth.

This simple model outlined in Isaiah is truly the heart of God's original design for how every metron should be stewarded and every garden cultivated. As we have seen in the garden model, the Lord desired that this would be a close, loving, family enterprise. He longs for us to live out this pattern every day and in every context. Through personal relationship

God imparts to teachable and humble children the manifold wisdom of God. Through his church, his family, his bride, he intends to bless not only the nations but every area of responsibility that is entrusted to mankind. The person who learns the "ways" of the Lord has become a carrier of the source code of heaven.

The manifold wisdom of God is the true source code of heaven uncorrupted, pure and perfectly designed to run on God's hardware. Your mandate is to behold the Lord, learn the manifold wisdom of God, and then beautifully guide and shape your garden. Jesus prayed, "Your kingdom come, your will be done, on earth as it is in heaven." (Matthew 6:10) A properly stewarded garden or metron will have the honor of being a part of the answer to Jesus' prayer. Remember, in God's original design, you look like your father and, your garden looks like you.

Corrupted Code

Every person, every metron, and every culture is afflicted by corrupted source code. Source code is the original design or foundation that all layers of software are built from in a computer system. *Culture is the software, and creation is God's hardware.* We, as the body of Christ, are called to co-labor with God to see the software of heaven operating in the hardware of creation. The manifold wisdom of God is the source code of heaven. This source code transforms nations so that their reality becomes more like heaven's reality — on earth as it is in heaven.

A way of illustrating this transformational mandate is to view your position in the kingdom equation as God's programmers. The mandate to the Church is to become master "code writers" who can re-code every broken area in your metron. We are entrusted with overwriting the existing code that was hacked by sin and now is swarming with viruses. The combination of the sin and destruction that fallen man and fallen angels have introduced onto God's perfect platform of creation, has enacted the biggest hack in history. The corrupted code or "virus" that was introduced and is still being injected through sin has been devastating to God's original design. Because rebellion and destruction are still at work, we keep busy with our father's business of reconciliation and restoration.

The devastating effects of corrupted code have been obvious since the original sin of Adam and Eve. The door that sin opened into God's perfect system led to the degradation of creation and the death of all things. The authority mankind handed over to the enemy gave him the ability to alter the source code and make things on earth not as they are in heaven. The devil began to overwrite the code of heaven using his new allies.

Then humans began to implement his operating system, called the "kingdom of the air" in Ephesians 2:2. Corruption, sin, death, and destruction were introduced like a virus into God's perfectly designed creation because humans aligned with the enemy. But God had a perfect plan to accomplish the "restoration of all things."

Fixing Code

Fixing the broken code of this world is a disruptive yet redemptive process. Along with your father God, you get the privilege of overwriting the broken and corrupted "code" that the enemy has introduced into creation.

"But the things which God announced beforehand by the mouth of all the prophets, that his Christ would suffer, he has thus fulfilled. Repent and return, so that your sins may be wiped away, in order that times of refreshing may come from the presence of the Lord; and that he may send Jesus, the Christ appointed for you, whom heaven must receive until the period ["Times" or "Periods"] of restoration of all things about which God spoke by the mouth of his holy prophets from ancient time."(Acts 3:18–21)

Acts 3 outlines a beautiful redemptive process which God has ordained to accomplish the full restoration of all things.

1. Christ suffered and died for our sins (propitiation)
2. We can "Repent and Return" (salvation — reconciliation)
3. So that "Our sins are wiped away" (justification)
4. "Times of refreshing may come" (reform)
5. "Times of Restoration" (transformation — process)
6. "All things" (culmination — at the great and glorious day of the return of Christ)

All peoples, nations, and aspects of your metron find themselves somewhere in this redemptive process. The majority of believers are fairly aware of the first three points in this process and are actively pursuing or at least supportive of seeing these processes accomplished in the world around them. Many do not have a paradigm that can also accommodate points 4 and 5. Recent spiritual and theological instruction has caused us to focus on points 1,2,3 then skip to 6. If we as the body of Christ are actually going to see the daily fulfillment of the Lord's Prayer, "Your kingdom come, your will be done on earth as it is in heaven" … then we also need to focus on points 4 and 5.

What would it look like to also include points 4 and 5? Let's look at the impact a holistic and transformationally minded believer can have on their sphere of influence or "metron."

Your co-laboring with Christ is the very work of rewriting the software that manages your metron. The manifold wisdom that you acquire in the presence and word of God is pure and flawless source code. Your metron, even if it's only you initially, is in desperate need of being restored. Through the Church (you), there is hope for every failed system. There is hope for every deceived individual. There is hope for transformation in every culture immersed in a source code corrupted by its false god.

The church is to manifest the culture of heaven in every sphere of influence in such a way that even the authorities in heavenly realms, i.e., the enemy and his forces, are forced to see that the wisdom of the Lord is high above all else. There is only one true God. The design that brings victory in all things is a submitted body of believers who seek God, learn his ways, acquire wisdom, then spread out and "heavenize" their sphere, garden, or metron. The body of believers is entrusted with the source code of heaven through our access to the throne of God. We meaningfully connect with the Lord and have access to the gifts of wisdom and understanding as promised in scripture. Scripture says that if we seek wisdom and understanding, we will find it. Wisdom and understanding flow from relationship with God and empower and commission us to creatively write code according to the culture of heaven.

The presence, power, and wisdom of God that flows through a believer like rivers of living water will ultimately silence the arrogant claims of the devil. As the followers of Christ intentionally reconnect their metron to the throne of God, kindness, and the blessings of the Lord will overwhelm all human argument against the character and nature of the Lord. We will see the enemy forced to concede. He will ultimately concede that Jesus Christ is Lord and that the ways of God are infinitely superior. He will acknowledge that the Author of wisdom has no equal.

End Game

"Then comes the end, when he delivers the kingdom to God the Father after destroying every rule and every authority and power. For he must reign until he has put all his enemies under his feet. The last enemy to be destroyed is death." (1 Corinthians 15:24—26 ESV)

After Christ's resurrection, he invited us to rule and reign with him. Ultimately the kingdom project culminates when all of Christ's enemies are abolished having been subdued. The true end game is when Christ hands over the completed kingdom project to the Father.

People are empowered when they have purpose. The body of Christ plays an integral role in God's redemptive plan for all of creation. A great sense of purpose is found in this process, and when our hope is in his ultimate victory. Every believer is commissioned to cultivate the culture of heaven into their sphere of influence. Every area in your metron can be kissed by heaven and brought to life, watered by the streams of living water that flows from your soul. Every metron can become like the Garden of Eden that hosts the presence of God, where people can behold the creator and become like him.

By this point in our study, we have begun to uncover a broader understanding of the Gospel and salvation. Remember, you are being saved to something not just saved from something. You matter and your metron matters.

Chapter 22

Occupy

*"Then the Lord God took the man and put him into the gar-
den of Eden to cultivate it and keep it."*(Genesis 2:15)

WE HAVE SEEN A VITAL NARRATIVE IN scripture called the Original Commission. The call to work is given to Adam and Eve in this commission.
This original commission is consistently affirmed as the source of mankind's identity and purpose throughout history. We have explored in detail
the first element of vocation found in Genesis 2:15, the word *abad* or
"cultivate." From this comes the understanding that work is fundamentally
spiritual; it is worship and of intrinsic eternal value. We also explored how
worship ultimately forms culture and how we have a mandate to bring the
culture of heaven into our metrons on earth. As part of God's family business, we embrace our commission along with Adam, Eve, Noah, Abraham,
Israel, and Jesus.

To be about our father's *business*, we are to multiply, spread out, and subdue (steward) creation. Co-laboring with the Holy Spirit in your metron
you become part of the answer to the prayer Jesus taught us to pray, "Your
kingdom come, your will be done, on earth as it is in heaven." In this, we
are moved to action.

We discovered that, like Adam and Eve, we all have a garden or a metron. The apostle Paul reaffirms this concept in 2 Corinthians 10:13 when
he indicates that he has a defined sphere of influence. Likewise, we have
come to understand that we have a delegated authority and responsibility
for a metron. In it, we co-author, with God, the software or culture that
characterizes a metron. Having looked at the word *abad*, which informs the
first element of vocation found in the Original Commission, we can shift
our focus to the second primary element in the commission, the word,

"keep." Exploring this equally important command to *keep* will lead many believers to a paradigm shift that answers two questions. "What do I do now that I believe?" and "What is the meaning of life in the here and now?"

The 2nd Element of Vocation

People often find that it is easier to attain to something than to retain it. In warfare it is generally much easier to take territory than it is to remake territory or retain what was gained. So it is with the cultivation in our metrons. The keeping of what has been gained requires stewardship. As we seek to obey the command to *keep*, we discover the mandate for occupation. Successfully obeying God's command to spread out and fill the earth requires active stewardship if it is to be subdued and the progress retained. In the Kingdom of God, the subduing and keeping happens through the work of our hands in the metron God has given. We are called to cultivate *and* keep.

> *"Work is a call of God upon an individual's life. It becomes the sphere through which, not merely in which, a Christian serves Christ and his kingdom. It is the occupation — the [21]principal business of one's life — through which one occupies territory or a sphere of influence (Luke 19:13) for Jesus Christ."* (Darrow Miller)

> *"But before leaving, he called in ten servants and gave each of them some money. He told them, 'Use this to earn more money until I get back.'"* (Luke 19:13 CEV)

When the King returns, he is expecting a return on his investment from us. Remember, it's not about the size or profile of the work we do in our metron but the faithfulness with which we steward or keep our master's property. We are all given a resource to manage. It may be the government of a nation, the hearts of your children or the spiritual atmosphere of a prison in which you find yourself incarcerated. All of us are accountable for the metron we occupy.

---

21 *Darrow Miller, LifeWork, page 9 Developing a Biblical Theology of Vocation Copyright © 2002 by Darrow L. Miller Published by the Disciple Nations Alliance*

The Purpose of Vocation

"'God doesn't call his people to be awesome or to be amazingly impactful,' he said. 'Every job is supremely important; anything that's creative, restorative or protective is an aspect of the image of God in us and how God has uniquely wired us and created us to serve the world and bless the world.'" (Scott Sauls)[22]

This quote from Scott Sauls makes an important point. *We don't need to be awesome or amazing. We only need to be obedient and faithful.* That being said, like any father, God has hopes and dreams for your life. God aims to do awesome and amazing things through you. Everything you set your hand to do is supremely important in God's creation. No matter how seemingly insignificant something seems to be, every human vocation is intended to be filled with dignity. Every activity is an opportunity to worship God. Don't feel inadequate or insecure about the amount of responsibility that God has entrusted to you. It is clear that God intentionally chooses the weak and foolish things in this world confound the wise.

"Brothers and sisters, think of what you were when you were called. Not many of you were wise by human standards; not many were influential; not many were of noble birth. But God chose the foolish things of the world to shame the wise; God chose the weak things of the world to shame the strong. God chose the lowly things of this world and the despised things — and the things that are not — to nullify the things that are, so that no one may boast before him." (1 Corinthians 1:26–29 NIV)

When God calls you, he equips you. When God does incredible things through average people, he receives glory, and his ways are recognized as high above all else. The power, wisdom, and means come from him, yet he chooses you to do the job.

Your vocation is the means that God uses to hold the territory of the kingdom. You and others who have come before you have cultivated and expanded the territory of the King, but this territory needs to be preserved. It must be guarded, protected, and watched over.

Our Father loves and gives good gifts. He wants to bless the work of your hands. Now that we have explored the overview of the origi-

---

22 *Scott Sauls, Irresistible Faith: ChristianPost.com January 6th, 2019*

nal commission, the Luke 19 parable comes into clearer focus. The man of noble birth informs his servants that he is going away to establish his kingdom and that they should be about his business with his resources until he returns. When he returns with his kingdom established, he asks for an accounting of what his servants have done with all that he had given them. He wants to see the return on his investment. He also wants to determine who he can entrust with the larger responsibilities in his kingdom. I believe the bigger point of the parable is that God is looking for those he can trust and reward.

Those servants who demonstrated obedience and diligence expanded their metron. They faithfully co-labored with their master and increased the resources of his kingdom. For their actions, they were rewarded with more responsibility and trust in relative measure. The servant who increased his master's investment ten times was put in charge of ten cities. The servant who was irresponsible with his master's property and misrepresented the character and nature of his master was severely punished. Until the day of the Lord, we don't precisely know what reward is stored in eternity for those who faithfully manage their metron. But we know that we have a good father and he is looking to reward his children.

Through co-laboring with God, you are given the privilege of seeing order and blessing cultivated into creation. Much of the mandate to *abad* is what we could describe as a countable or quantitative activity within your metron. You may be building, designing, or establishing something that did not exist before. Through connecting with the wisdom of God, you may be putting forward thought leadership and solutions in government. Your connection to the original artist may produce, through you, beauty and meaning that remind people of the beauty of God.

Someone's work in scientific and medical fields might bring hope and solutions to the broken areas of your metron. Decisions you make as a leader can be infused with wisdom and knowledge from the courts of heaven. Your calling as a parent or spouse can bring the living water of unconditional love, acceptance, and trust into your family. You are commissioned to cultivate the source code of heaven into the chaos of creation. You carry the authority and mandate to displace the chaos, oppression, and darkness in your metron. No work of darkness is safe from the believer who knows their authority and acts on their commission in the kingdom.

No matter the scope or nature of your vocation, a believer is also called to *keep* what has been cultivated. According to Genesis 2:15, there is a mandate to guard, protect, and watch over. The mandate to keep is nicely balanced with the mandate to cultivate. Meaning and grandeur are restored to your vocation when the command to *keep* is embraced. In exploring the word *shamar*, our vision will be broadly expanded.

Called to Keep

"Then the Lord God took the man and put him into the garden of Eden to culti-vate it and keep it."(Genesis 2:15)

The word *keep*, translated from the word Hebrew *shamar* means "to guard, protect, and watch over." [23] It is in exploring the implications of the word *shamar* that things get truly exciting! Here we dive into new dimensions of what it means to be a Christian who embraces the original commission!

Much useful thought and Bible exposition have been offered regarding the concepts of vocation and work as worship. Customarily the initial approach is focused on developing good spiritual disciplines and character development, being successful spiritually and personally. The next level of focus rightly tends towards representing God well in one's personal and work life. I see these approaches as tactical and practical. This study has aimed to take a close look into the supernatural framework that underpins the tactical and practical. We explored the strategic and big-picture perspective of vocation. In the first part of this study, we have explored the concept of work as worship and the spiritual roots of culture. We saw that work, worship, and the management of culture are core responsibilities for every believer. The goal is to create a framework of theology to support everything in life.

In this journey to understand our original commission, we now add another Rosetta Stone or key to these understandings. The *shamar* concept is central to fulfilling this commission and especially to understanding the depth of trust that God has placed in you. I have seen very little attention

---

23 *Strong's Concordance #H8104*

paid to this second key — *shamar*. This idea equally defines the original commission. In the original commission, the word *abad* or "cultivate" is the first imperative. The second imperative is the often-overlooked word "keep."

Gaining a good understanding of how the word keep or *shamar* was originally used will open up your eyes to the immensity of God's kingdom project. The implications of this idea also expand your metron job description. It broadens the scope of work far beyond that which most believers perceive. Along with this new depth of understanding regarding your commission comes a deep realization that God wants to trust you. He wants you to walk and work with him every day on everything in his kingdom. We have explored the first element of vocation which is to cultivate your metron. But how does one keep a metron?

Shamar is an action word; it is a verb. *Shamar* was also a functional aspect of the job description that a priest fulfilled in Jewish tradition and throughout Scripture. A good word study of the word *shamar* reveals its meaning as, "To exercise great care over something." Also contained in it are the ideas of creating and maintaining a *hedge* around something to protect it and to actively guard against intruders. *Tending* is also an identified layer of meaning. The concept of tending to something is closely aligned with our understanding of management or stewardship.

Adam and Eve were called to be royal priests in their garden temple. Now we, as the new priesthood of believers, are called to serve as priests in our garden temples. The apostle Peter writes about this high calling and our identity as royal priests under the new covenant.

"But you are a chosen race, a royal priesthood, a holy nation, a people for God's own possession, so that you may proclaim the excellencies of him who has called you out of darkness into his marvelous light." (1 Peter 2:9)

You may have a certain mental picture of what a priest is and what they do. Often we think of them wearing robes and performing rituals. The Old Testament priesthood was an exclusive role that had the aim of mediating and managing the two-way connection between God and Man. The priest was responsible for ministering to the Lord through worship and ritual. Priests also mediated the relationship of mankind with God through teaching, guiding, and managing the connection point. Under the old covenant, the connection point was deep inside the temple — in the holy of holies.

Now, in the new covenant, we should think of priests wearing work boots, suits, raincoats, and carrying computers or boxes of supplies. These are just as significant and supernatural as the amulets of the ancient priests. Not only are you a royal priest in your metron as described above, but you are also a mobile temple!

What is inside the temple? The very presence of God, the Holy Spirit. The Spirit of God is longing to manifest through you with every strike of the hammer or click of a computer. Your metron cannot escape your influence. The only question is what will be the source of the code that you are using to shape what you influence. Remember that what is inside you will shape the world around you. This is the design of God's kingdom; it is internal to external. It is an influence, not an imposition. Who will be worshiped, and what culture will be established within your metron? Answering this question is within your scope of responsibility.

In the new covenant, the royal priesthood still serves to cultivate worship as the connection point between heaven and earth. But now the robes become work clothes, and the rituals become vocations. This quote from Abraham Kuyper serves to reinforce the magnitude of our position as a co-laborer with God in his kingdom.

"Wherever man may stand, whatever he may do, to whatever he may apply his hand, in agriculture, in commerce, and in industry or his mind, in the work of art, and science, in whatsoever it may be, he is constantly standing before the face of God, he is employed in the service of his God, he has strictly to obey his God, and above all, he has to aim at the glory of his God."[24]

Let's return to exploring the second element of vocation—to keep. It is important to note the first location of this word in Genesis. In scripture, the first time a word or concept is employed is vital to how it is interpreted or viewed in later scriptural uses.

This first mention and context of *shamar* becomes an interpretive lens through which we understand the meaning of the word or concept when it appears later in scripture. When God gives the original commission and instructs Adam to cultivate and keep the garden, he is saying that Adam was to *shamar*. Adam and Eve received a two-part commission, and we

---

24 *Abraham Kuyper. Lectures on Calvinism, (Grand Rapids, Mich.:Wm. B. Eerdmans Publishing Co., 1983) 53*

have received these same mandates. I have described them as the first and second elements of vocation. Since a proper understanding of *shamar* is critical to our attempt to build a framework theology of vocation, we need to take a deeper look at this mandate. Let's take a look at the outline of uses and meanings found in the Brown, Briggs, Gesenius Lexicon.

Definition: *Shamar*

1. to keep, guard, observe, give heed
2. to keep, have charge of to keep, guard, keep watch and ward, protect, save life

watch, watchman (participle)

1. to watch for, wait for
2. to watch, observe
3. to keep, retain, treasure up (in memory)
4. to keep (within bounds), restrain
5. to observe, celebrate, keep (sabbath or covenant or commands), perform (vow)
6. to keep, preserve, protect
7. to keep, reserve

For our purposes, I summarize these into a working definition of *shamar*: guard, protect, and watch over.

Kingdom Metrics

You can see from the meaning found in the word *shamar* that the original commission was a deep and open-ended mandate. When Adam and Eve were instructed to multiply, fill the earth and subdue it, there was a spiritual and a natural aspect to the commission. Both the spiritual and natural conditions found in the garden were to be cultivated and kept.

We all long to serve and please our Father God, and for us to lean into our purpose in the kingdom, we must understand our full mandate. As with any job description, we need to know the expected scope of work. Otherwise, how will we know if we are succeeding?

As we look at the mandates contained in the original commission, I propose that we see coequal *quantitative* and *qualitative* elements within the scope of work. It is possible to identify two metrics in the original commission. The metrics of the original commission are expansion or growth and quality assurance. These are the key responsibilities in managing your metron.

Let's look at the definition of these kingdom metrics.

Quantitative: This word relates to or involves the measurement of quantity or amount. Something is quantitative when it can be counted. (Expansion and Growth)

Qualitative: This word relates to or involves quality. Something is qualitative when it relates to the quality, character, or nature of something. (Quality Assurance)

Within our commission we are not only to take ground through multiplication, subduing and cultivation but also to hold the ground. The build quality within the kingdom does matter.

We are not necessarily talking about a natural understanding of taking or holding ground in the physical sense. The Kingdom of God expands outward through the innermost being of each person who willingly submits to the Lordship of Christ. His lordship in your life starts as a "mustard seed" then grows into an enormous tree of life. The smallest of seeds becomes a blessing to your metron and the scope of your influence. Correct spiritual alignment inside you inevitably produces increasing alignment within your metron between heaven and earth. The Kingdom of God is within you. You are a mobile temple filled with the Holy Spirit. If Christ rules and reigns within you, then the kingdom has come and is coming… no part of your metron escapes the rivers of living water. The mustard seed is growing and is expanding according to God's original design. The darkness around you will eventually be scoured away by the flow and pressure of living water. As your inner man is discipled and aligned with the Kingdom of God, you cannot help but pour in the atmosphere of heaven.

Quality Assurance

Just like Adam and Eve, we are called to steward all that God had created and all that is cultivated. We are to hold the ground and protect the culture that hosts the presence of God in our garden. We are to guard, protect, and watch over all that is established through our co-laboring with Christ. One primary way we hold the ground in our metron is to embrace the mandate of *quality assurance*. It is harder to evaluate qualitative aspects than quantitative.

Success with the qualitative often is related to managing processes and practices. Managing processes and practices are often considered the not so glamorous and less exciting aspect of one's work. People tend to resonate with visible or tangible results such as a completed product, a harvested crop, or an earned degree. But in the kingdom, how one arrives at the result matters to God just as much as the final accomplishment. Guarding, protecting and watching over processes and practices is very much within your *shamar* mandate in the kingdom. It is not a command for "special" Christians or for those that are in a particular religious vocation. To *keep* is a coequal command for all who cultivate.

Here are a few key indicators that may help you evaluate your *shamar* work:

- Do you protect the processes and practices that are at work in your metron?
- Is the presence of God evident in your actual work efforts?
- Do you watch over your source code and operating system that manages your metron?
- Is the culture of heaven consistently evident in you to those you influence?
- Do you value the quality of your work as much as accomplishing countable tasks?
- Are you as faithful with the little as with a large amount of responsibility?
- Do you value the godliness of the means to the end as much as the ends themselves?
- Do you constantly stay spiritually aware of guarding the gates to your garden?
- Do you endeavor to keep the rivers of living water flowing freely from within you into your metron?
- Do you regularly evaluate the condition of your metron against the benchmarks found in the written word of God?
- Do people experience a vacation in heaven when they interact with

your metron on earth?

* Do you see expansion and growth within your metron?

Another good way to understand the command to *keep* is to utilize
the word *tend*. Tending is the ongoing management that has much to do
with the eventual quality of outcomes. Numbers are important, and there
is much terrain that must be subdued and cultivated, but we must also
value the tending that ensures quality. The tending or management of the
ground that is taken both spiritually and naturally is part of the obedience
equation. Qualitative results matter just as much as the quantitative in the
kingdom. We must both *cultivate* and *keep*.

The role of guarding, protecting, and watching over what was cultivated
is the bottom line of stewardship. Within the original commission was an
aspect that was measurable by counting and an aspect that was measurable
by quality. God had given a holistic mandate to mankind to expand but also
to go deep. The deeper dimension of managing your metron is all about
quality. Most have found it is often easier to build something rather than to
maintain what was built.

Many armies have often won the battle but lost the war because they
could not hold the ground they took. This was a lesson learned the hard
way by the Roman Empire and led to the commissioning of the original
"apostles" as a military function. We explored this original concept of
Apostle and how the term was utilized by the church in the New Testament as a key functionary title. Historically, the Roman army apostle was
as much concerned about the quality and durability of Rome's expansion
as he was about the quantity of land that had been subdued. Similarly, we
as metron apostles must embrace the commission to keep and steward
the kingdom. To do this, we must daily keep in mind that we are called
to manage both key indicators in our metron. Our scope of work includes both the first and second elements of vocation found in the original
commission. Embracing the second element of vocation is to function as a
kingdom keeper or one who does the work of *shamar*.

Just as Adam's garden needed the work of *shamar*, your metron requires
quality assurance. Adam and Eve discovered that there were real threats
to God's creation. In the garden, there was a real snake, and there are real
snakes in your metron. Until Christ returns and fully establishes his rule
such threats will persist. Your family, work, community, environment,

health, relationship with God, economic well being, character and every other facet that comprises your metron will experience threats.

Remember that we are called to "reverse the effects of the fall," as Darrow Miller comments regarding the purpose of vocation. Reversing the effects of the fall means to actively countermand the enemy who aims to "kill, steal, and destroy."

We are called to be effective stewards. Managing your metron includes guarding, protecting against the threats so that the Lord will receive a return on his investment. We will be held accountable for the investment the King has entrusted to us. When you *abad* and *shamar*, you keep the devil out by filling all the available space in your metron with the presence and ways of God. Your vocation is the primary means through which you shape the world around you. As a member of the body of Christ, the Church, you can do this! You are promised access to the manifold wisdom of God! Your identity and the resources of heaven you have received are intended to be born out as solutions for Creation. When you go up to the mountain of the Lord (Isaiah 2:3) you then have something to offer to the broken world around you.

Chapter 23

Keep your Metron

THERE IS A CONSTANT STRUGGLE IN THE spiritual realm over who will control your metron. Part of the art of managing your metron is to maintain your delegated spiritual authority over what God has entrusted you. Consider the account of Jesus' temptation in the wilderness. We want to better to understand the consequences of Adam and Eve, giving their delegated authority to Satan.

> *"And he led him up and showed him all the kingdoms of the world in a moment of time. And the devil said to him, 'I will give you all this domain and its glory; for it has been handed over to me, and I give it to whomever I wish. Therefore if you worship before me, it shall all be yours.' Jesus answered him, 'It is written, "You shall worship the Lord your God and serve him only."'"* (Luke 4:5–8)

Satan appears well aware of Christ's aim to reclaim his dominion and Kingship over the world. He tempts Jesus with his own goals. He is essentially offering Jesus a way to reclaim his kingdom without the suffering and dying component. Satan tempts Jesus to take the easy way out with the requirement that he bends his knee in worship to Satan. Satan articulates that all authority over creation had been handed to him, by Adam, and that he had the authority to give it to whomever he wanted. Note the fact that Jesus did not dispute Satan's claims.

Satan would have been fine with giving Jesus all these *domains* and their *glory* as long as he got to keep his ultimate prize. He wanted to be worshiped as God. For Satan, the chance to be worshiped by God would be worth any trade-off. His original sin was his pride, and he was cast out of heaven for saying that he would be like God. Jesus' rebuke to Satan is about to whom worship will be given. Jesus essentially says, "No thanks," when he replies, "You shall worship the Lord your God and serve him only."

This response to temptation means that only God would receive worship. The enemy had what he wanted for a long season, and he is furious that he lost it. In his rush to destroy the son of God, he ended up being paraded in public like a fool. Remember that Colossians 2 simply says, "And having disarmed the powers (principalities) and authorities, he made a public spectacle of them, triumphing over them by the cross."

When you manage your metron, you will find that the enemy wants to deceive you into serving him. He wants your metron back, and he wants to deceive you into handing it over.

"For he must reign until he has put all his enemies under his feet." (1 Corinthians 15:25 NIV)

The kingdom truly is now but is still coming to future completeness. It has already happened, it is happening to us, and the success of Christ's Kingdom project will further humiliate the devil. We are co-laboring with God to subdue the "enemies" of the King. The management of metrons is often like being a spiritual sheriff over a jurisdiction that is crawling with snakes and scorpions. We know our battle is not against flesh and blood but against spiritual powers and authorities in heavenly places. Spiritual enemies are the first that we are to *keep* out of our garden. As we rightly order the spiritual environment, we find that our natural environment easily comes into right order.

There are still snakes trying to corrupt his kingdom, but they have to get past those that *keep*. But take heart. Scripture assures us that Jesus works in and through us until the culmination of his kingdom.

"...then comes the end, when he hands over the kingdom to the God and Father, when he has abolished all rule and all authority and power." (1 Corinthians 15:24)

His return will truly be the great and glorious day of the Lord! Until this time we fight, we cultivate, and we keep.

It is the long-term vision that gives us hope. We are intricately woven into the redemptive story of the Kingdom of God. The fulfilling of our commissions to *abad* and *shamar* bring us meaning and purpose. The kingdom process we are invited into as co-heirs with Christ Jesus truly gives us the chance to walk in the garden with the Lord.

In this kingdom journey, we are building to last. We are subduing the chaos that is found all around us through reproducing the heavenly culture that is manifest in our hearts. Effective stewardship over one's metron requires not only the quantitative work found in the original commission but also the qualitative work of *shamar*.

Remember, in the original commission, God gave Adam and Even authority as well as responsibility. Successful quality assurance requires us to understand our delegated authority. We are to constantly exercise that spiritual authority to regulate what influences are allowed into our metron. The failure of Adam's son Cain is a cautionary tale for all of us. Through God's interaction with Cain we are reminded that there is always a serpent trying to introduce *corrupted code* into the relationship between God and his creation.

Look at what God said to Cain in Genesis when he warns him about his behavior and choices.

"If you do not do well, sin is crouching at the door; and its desire is for you, but you must master it." (Genesis 4:7b)

This is valuable wisdom for all who aim to steward their metron well. Remember, as the one to whom God has delegated the *authority of shamar;* you become the gatekeeper to your metron. Adam was commissioned to guard the gate of the garden, and you are commissioned to guard the gate of your sphere of influence. Failure to *shamar* or keep our garden has massive implications as Adam and Eve were the first to discover.

To protect the garden from the source code of darkness, Adam and Eve were expelled from their sphere of influence. God cares about creation, and he moved immediately to position an angel and a flashing sword to cut off corrupted mankind from accessing the tree of life in the garden. Mankind's influence had been compromised, and God immediately moved to limit their influence.

For success to be authentic, there must be an opportunity for real failure. Failure is always an option it would seem. When Adam and Eve sinned, they were expelled from the garden. The previous depths of relationship with God had been broken, and their job of cultivating and keeping the culture of heaven connected to earth became intensely more difficult. They were no longer able to access the pure *source code of heaven* and manifest that on earth. Their sin had subjugated them to the wrong kingdom, and their God-given authority had been turned over to the enemy.

You are in the family business whether you know it or not. Our father's business is the business of reconciliation and the restoration of all things. Co-laboring with Christ is the heart of our day to day vocation and the source of our purpose and meaning in life. We are called to move in the opposite spirit of the works of darkness and endeavor to strengthen the nations through our vocation.

God is looking for men and women who will take their vocation seriously. Anyone who despises natural work within their metron as *unspiritual* is aligning with the one who weakens the nations. You will extend your influence to the degree that you treat everything you do as an eternity shaping act of significance. The story of the Old Testament becomes the story of God searching for men and women who reconnect with God and then based on right relationship, rule on earth. God made it clear that if mankind would repent and turn from following idols, there was the hope of restoration and redemption.

Earlier, we noted that there were history-making moments when God co-labored with righteous individuals. These moments in spiritual history pointed towards the coming Kingdom of God. Adam, Eve, Noah, Abraham, David, and many others became leading indicators of God's original design. To some degree, they all embraced the original commission. When Jesus inaugurated his kingdom on earth, the liberation of all of creation was at hand. When Jesus meets with his disciples just before his departure, he made clear the outcome of his death and resurrection.

"And Jesus came up and spoke to them, saying, 'All authority has been given to Me in heaven and on earth.'" (Matthew 28:18)

The kingdom is here. Now go and build the kingdom.

A Spiritually Resilient Metron

"nor give place to the devil." (Ephesians 4:27 NKJV)

The best approach to keeping the snakes out of your metron is to not allow room for them in the first place. By maintaining the spiritual space within your own heart and metron, you fill the space so full of the presence and ways of God that the enemy finds no opportunity.

Ideally, the minute he tries to raise his head or speak a word of deception, his lies are identified, and the truth crushes him. You don't have to constantly worry about the snakes if you know that your walls are maintained. The environment of your garden, if cultivated with the Lord, becomes repellent to the kingdom of this world. A spiritually resilient metron is one that has an atmosphere so filled with the presence of God that any darkness that slips in is naturally displaced.

Like oil and water, the two kingdoms cannot cohabitate the same space. Essentially displacement is the removal of a lesser force by a greater force within a given space. Remember, greater is he that is in you than he that is in the world. Transformation is a great example of displacement. A disciple of Christ is one who has been transformed by the renewing of the mind.

"And do not be conformed to this world, but be transformed by the renewing of your mind, so that you may prove what the will of God is, that which is good and acceptable and perfect." (Romans 12:2)

A spiritually resilient metron can only be achieved if you as *cultivator* and *keeper* have a transformed mind. When you are faced with a choice, do you conform to the software of this world system, or do you renew your mind? Transformation is what happens when a believer chooses to connect with the source code of heaven and reject the temptation to align with the counterfeit code of the kingdom of darkness. The command given in Romans 12 is not related to one's individual salvation. The message was given to believers. Essentially the author is giving instructions to the church as to what comes next. After you believe and are saved, then what do you do?

You pursue transformation by the renewing of your mind. Also important is the reason indicated for transformation—that you may prove what the will of God is. If you do things God's way, in God's universe, it will work. To effectively carry out the work of quality assurance in your metron, you must have benchmarks. Romans 12:2 provides three benchmark metrics. The good, acceptable, and perfect. These are just an example of the source code of heaven that can transform your metron. By the transformation that comes with the renewing of your mind, this code of heaven is proved to be good, acceptable, and perfect.

Transformation is a progressive and living process. We go through various stages and levels of renewing throughout life, and eventually, we will be complete when we are in our fully resurrected bodies. To see transformation in your metron start by being transformed in your mind. This transformation is how you cultivate and keep your connection between heaven and your metron. Let's explore one key mechanism of transformation to help us better grasp this process.

Transformation can be defined as the displacement of ideas, beliefs, practices, and values (worldview) that originate in *darkness* with the ideas, beliefs, practices, and values that emanate from the person of God.

Displacement and transformation are both fruits of cultivation and keeping. Transformation of the mind is the work of displacing corrupted source code and replacing it with the source code of heaven. This is not only the standing command for the people of God. It is the aim of your metron management.

Keeping the snakes out of your metron is much the same as keeping viruses out of a computer system. If your software system begins to falter and the hardware (creation) is not performing as designed, then you immediately check for viruses. The issues are usually predictable and fixable. Viruses, corrupted code, compatibility issues, incomplete software updates, hacking, and outright attacks are regular offenders.

All of these variables can be controlled and resolved by an effective IT manager. Spiritual snakes often attempt to exploit any opportunity to influence the system or culture of your metron. The faithful steward is watching for these intrusions and vulnerabilities and is co-laboring with Christ to manage the Father's business. Managing your metron well is important to God and the people and realms of creation that God has entrusted to you.

The enemy will creep into any unguarded space and attempt to own it. If allowed to stay he will. If undetected, he will influence. To see incredible change in the natural world, displace the spiritual reality that seeks to destroy. If you don't identify and counter the enemy, he will continually seek to poison your metron by injecting the wrong source code. He may not find a way to do it through you if you have aligned yourself with Christ's kingdom. But, he will regularly test your attentiveness. He will probe your defenses and seeks an undetected way in even if he has been previously displaced.

He knows he can't win an open and obvious confrontation with you since you are filled with the Holy Spirit and are living the scriptural promise that "greater is he that is in you than he that is in the world." In the name of Jesus, you have victory over the snakes and scorpions as promised in scripture. Jesus describes how the enemy tries to get back into a position of influence in a person even after he has been removed.

The gospel writer Luke records Jesus describing this reality.

"When the unclean spirit goes out of a man, it passes through waterless places seeking rest, and not finding any, it says, 'I will return to my house from which I came.' And when it comes, it finds it swept and put in order. Then it goes and takes along seven other spirits more evil than itself, and they go in and live there; and the last state of that man becomes worse than the first." (Luke 11:24–26)

To hold the spiritual ground in your metron, you must *intentionally* occupy. The one who has been set free of spiritual pollution and bondage must fill the open space to keep out snakes. Scripture intends us to realize that the presence of God must take up residence in the individual who is delivered from the enemy lest that same enemy returns with seven worse than himself and sets up shop again. When your metron is swept clean and put in order, you must make sure that the air of heaven remains the source of the spiritual atmosphere.

Cultivation is the key to growing a new culture within your sphere of influence. If you cultivate a new ecosystem that is fed by the streams of living water flowing from heaven, you will find that there is no room left for the enemy in that same space. A metron that is left without diligent tending and keeping will inevitably be reclaimed by an old and opportunistic enemy. When a garden is left untended, it becomes a place of chaos, weeds, trespassers, and fruitlessness. Your metron will be like that if you don't contend for its condition.

Indeed, there is a very real role for *quality assurance* in the Kingdom of God. The work of tending and keeping is part of your commission whether your scope of influence is limited to the garden of your own attitude or you are cultivating the world view of an entire nation. All of these considerations are make or break to managing your metron in the kingdom of God.

Chapter 24

Metrons and Mission

IN ADDITION TO THE 1ST AND 2ND elements of vocation (cultivate) and (keep), there is a 3rd element that closes the loop in our exploration of work, mission and meaning in this study. The third element of vocation is that managing your metron automatically puts you "on mission."

It may seem strange to those in the body of Christ who are not working in traditional, vocational ministry roles to consider yourself a missionary, but it is true. As a metron manager, you are called to be the cultural apostle with the responsibility to bring the culture of heaven into your sphere of influence. The Roman Empire's military apostle was a *sent one* going to a conquered region to "romanize" all areas of the new territory. You also are a "sent one" bringing the gospel and presence of God into every area of your metron. It is likely that within all of your spheres of influence are uncultivated areas that have not been cultured, kept, protected, and watched over.

You might be saying, "I am not a missionary." But if we view any vocation at any phase in life, through the lens of the original commission we find mission.

Mission?

Let's first get a clear understanding of the definition and origin of the word. The word "mission" originated in the English language from the Latin word *missio*. *Missio* originated from the Latin *mittere*, which means *send or sent*. Its common Christian use is traced back to the work of the Jesuit workers who went around the world as the first recorded, organized *missionary* effort. The Oxford English Dictionary comments that the word denoted the "sending of the Holy Spirit into the world."

This original use of the word mission, with the idea of sending the Holy Spirit into the world, is particularly relevant to our entire study on vocation and the original commission. Bringing the ways and presence of God, into an area where it is not known, is by definition, *missional*.

In addition to the dynamics of expansion found in God's original design, we say that there is the often-overlooked command to *keep* what has been cultivated. Keeping can be accurately thought of as actively guarding and protecting. By guarding and protecting, one can "hold the ground." To hold the ground of your garden you have to occupy the available space. The atmosphere must be spiritually filled by heaven. Either the Holy Spirit will define the atmosphere, via your connection with heaven, or the enemy will extend his influence. Either way your metron will be spiritually occupied. The spirit occupying that space will govern the physical condition of the world around you. I suggest that occupying is the work of *shamar* and is largely done within the context of your vocation. Your work, your vocation, is entirely significant, and being on mission in your metron is essential.

On Mission

When looking at the Great Commission given by Jesus in the New Testament, many Christians might say, "That command is something *other* people are called to do." Too often it is thought that mission, the Great Commission, is work for the *spiritual* or *special* Christ-followers to accomplish. It is quite easy to fall into the habit of separating our regular life activities and vocation into the secular box while assigning the spiritual activities such as missions or vocational ministry, into the *sacred* box.

Our constant temptation is to live as functional gnostics. It is too easy to align your view of work with the heresy of Gnosticism rather than the Kingdom of God. The original design was for the kingdom to be an integrated reality. This was illustrated in the Garden of Eden. In the garden, there was no sacred and secular dichotomy.

In salvation, you are transferred into the Kingdom of God and commissioned to build the kingdom. If the Great Commission is for every believer then every believer is a sent one. Jesus would not give a reality defining command to all believers unless there was a way for all believers to obey. Obedience to the Great Commission is a path that runs through the middle of your metron.

The work of mission is found in the very heart of the original commission. If you are committed to fulfilling the original commission, you will naturally find yourself functioning as a missionary. It is in the job description of everyone who manages their metron.

The Great ReCommission

"And Jesus came up and spoke to them, saying, "All authority has been given to Me in heaven and on earth. Go therefore and make disciples of all the nations, baptizing them in the name of the Father and the Son and the Holy Spirit, teaching them to observe all that I commanded you; and lo, I am with you always, even to the end of the age." (Matthew 28:18–20)

Looking closely at the Great Commission, we see clear parallels between the *Original Commission* and the *Great Commission*. These parallels are stunning. The Great Commission is so similar to the Original Commission that it could be described as the *Great Recommission*.

From the Great Commission, we embrace the commission to; Go, Make Disciples, Baptize, Teach them to Observe. The first three elements are fairly straight forward and are generally countable. These are the "quantitative" metrics of the kingdom earlier discussed. The element that is not adequately understood is this word *observe* in verse 20. This word is translated from the Greek word *téreó*.[25] The phonetic spelling is *tay-reh'-o*.

Exploring the word *téreó* (observe/obey) in the Great Commission will cause a sea change in understanding what it means to be on mission. I believe that the restoration of dignity and purpose to the majority of the body of Christ hinges on properly appreciating the mandate of *téreó*.

As with the original commission, the Great Commission contains both quantitative and qualitative commands. It is the quantitative part of the Great Commission with which most missional believers are familiar. First,

---

25 *Strong's Concordance #G5083*

there is the command to *go*. It is connected to the origins of the word *mission*. The command to *go* inherently conveys the idea of movement or initiative.

The next quantitative command is to make disciples. You can count how many disciples are made since it is numerically quantifiable. Then we see the command to "baptize." This command element is also numerically quantifiable. The vast majority of protestant Christian mission thinking and practice has been centered around the quantitative elements of the Great Commission. When you think of *mission work*, you likely picture evangelism, church planting, preaching, plus relief, and development efforts. This is why we often hear the work of the Great Commission described as a task. The quantitative aspects of the commission are countable or quantifiable, and this overemphasis on the quantifiable has led many to believe that we can complete the Great Commission. The quantifiable elements of the Great Commission might be suitably approached as a task. But the second element can only be fulfilled as an ongoing, open-ended way of life.

Often the understanding of mission has been weakened by not engaging the qualitative command to "teach them to observe." This is what I refer to as the second part of the Great Commission. Traditionally, obedience to the Great Commission has been limited to a focus on what you can count, or what is quantitative. Approaching the Great Commission through the lens of the *Original Commission*, we encounter a deeper mandate. The second half of the Great Commission is all about teaching disciples to guard, protect, and watch over all that is commanded and all that is cultivated. What was commanded to Adam in the original commission is mandated to believers in the Great Commission.

Managing your metron is all about the work of *shamar*. The Great Commission actually reaffirms this by commissioning you to teach what you can reach. The command *shamar* and *téreó* are the qualitative aspects of the Great Commission.

You may have heard terms such as "Discipling Nations." This concept is rooted in the idea that the qualitative element of the Great Commission is equal to the quantitative element. Look at the definition of the Greek word *téreó*—the under-emphasized part of the Great Commission.

Téreó
Definition: to watch over, to guard
Usage: I keep, guard, observe, watch over

Does this sound familiar? The definition of keep or *shamar* in the Original Commission is equivalent to the word observe or *téreó*.

Shamar
Definition: to keep, guard, observe, give heed
Usage: to keep, have charge of to keep, guard, keep watch, ward, protect, save life

The Great Commission was not a new idea. Jesus restated the original commission to his people! There are quantitative and qualitative elements in the original commission. We find these same elements in the Great Commission.

Shamar and *téreó* not only share a common meaning, but the implications are also commonly underemphasized or completely overlooked. We now see that God has had the same plan and the same method of operation in mind since he created mankind. He cares about quantity, and he cares about quality. Work in the kingdom is both wide and deep.

In the interwoven nature of the original commission and the Great Commission, how shall we frame a holistic understanding of mission? I believe you can view the commissions as two sides of the same coin. Like a coin, mission has two sides that present two aspects of the same whole. To manage your metron in the kingdom, you must value and fulfill both sides of the mission. Place equal importance on both sides of the coin. One side indicates the value of quantity and the other of quality. Here are a few key examples of the equivalency found on different sides of the same kingdom coin.

- Reach and Teach
- Evangelize and Disciple
- Quantity and Quality
- Width and Depth
- Subdue and Occupy
- *Abad* and *Shamar*
- Go and Stay
- Width and Depth
- Expansion and Permanence
- Cultivate and Keep

Make Disciples who Make it Right

Jesus' final earthly command to his disciples was that they go and make more disciples. They were to make disciples who were taught to *téreó* all that Christ had commanded. The Great Commission is interpreted as a universal commandment to all those that would claim Christ. A disciple is one who in his obedience guards, protects and watches over the culture of the kingdom that Jesus' actions and words established.

One could evaluate one's kingdom self-identity according to a new paradigm — one based on an expanded understanding of being a disciple. Some have understood the concept of *disciple* to be limited to areas of personal spiritual growth or study of the Bible. While these are key aspects of discipleship, the expansive nature of stewarding creation requires us to expand our perspective. Take a fresh look at the nature of a disciple who is commissioned to manage a metron.

- A disciple — one who follows and emulates another, they are teachable.
- A disciple is first a redeemed follower of Christ and in turn, desires that all men would be saved.
- Disciples are those who have become what they have beheld; their eyes have been fixed on God, and they have been transformed by the renewing of their minds.
- A truly discipled believer will have beheld the Lord and becomes like him.
- A disciple pursues wisdom from the Lord through the promised access to the manifold wisdom of God.
- For a disciple in the kingdom, there is no sacred and secular divide in their heart. One thing is not elevated as spiritual above another that is labeled natural. They are not professing Christians who are practicing gnostics.
- Disciples have an appreciation for "all things" and recognize the image of God in all of creation.
- Disciples embrace the eternal value of vocation and thrive in their calling to occupy.
- The disciple is one who has laid hold of their identity in Christ and confidently uses the manifold wisdom of God to manage their metron. Their aim is to manage it all just as if it was the throne room of

heaven.

- A disciple realizes that the world around them was designed to require mankind to be cultivated and kept in a manner that would suit the King.
- Disciples make every effort to displace the works of darkness and subdue the chaos and corruption in the world.
- The disciple is one who realizes that the presence of God resides in their inner being with the same intensity that the presence of God inhabited the ark of the covenant in the temples of ancient Israel.
- Disciples understand that the kingdom is where the King reigns and resides. Disciples operate as mobile temples of God and manage their connection point between heaven and earth.
- The disciple is one who recognizes they are part of a family business and that work is good and co-laboring with God is the means through which the kingdom is established.
- Disciples enthusiastically co-labor with God in any vocation to which they are called. They work from a place of favor — not for favor as they are already seated in heavenly places with Christ Jesus.
- Disciples embrace their appointment as cultural apostles who cultivate the ways of God and *code* every aspect of their metron.
- Disciples attentively guard, protect, and watch over everything that belongs to their father, and they teach others to do the same.
- Disciples embrace the Great Commission to include teaching disciples to expand, subdue, cultivate, and keep.
- The kingdom disciple recognizes that the condition of their metron is a manifestation of the spiritual condition inside them.
- Disciples live to see Jesus prayer answered: "May it be on earth as it is in heaven."
- Disciples make disciples who make things right.

Consider the example group of disciples in the early church who engaged in distinct obedience to the guidance of the Holy Spirit. There are those who are called into vocational ministry and those that are called to *occupy*.

The 3%

There is a percentage of believers who are called out by the Lord to work in full-time vocational ministry. Most believers are aware of these areas of unique calling. Positions and callings such as vocational pastor, missionary, teacher, evangelist, doing mercy ministry, and the many other ministries of the church universal.

It is estimated that 3% of the body of Christ could or would ever work vocationally in these capacities. 3% is a generous estimate as in actuality only .5 percent of believers are active in these types of vocational ministry roles. It is likely that another 2.5% are called but have not yet responded to the work the Lord has for them. This is why the work of seminaries, missionary mobilization, training, missionary sending, and vision casting are still vitally needed in the Church. Many believers have yet to obey and step out into the work to which they are called.

The Holy Spirit desires to set apart certain believers for the work of vocational ministry. The scriptural point of reference for how God calls members of the Church to work in a 3% capacity is found in Acts 13.

> *"Now there were at Antioch, in the church that was there, prophets and teachers: Barnabas, and Simeon who was called Niger, and Lucius of Cyrene, and Manaen who had been brought up with Herod the tetrarch, and Saul. While they were ministering to the Lord and fasting, the Holy Spirit said, 'Set apart for Me Barnabas and Saul for the work to which I have called them.' Then, when they had fasted and prayed and laid their hands on them, they sent them away. So, being sent out by the Holy Spirit, they went down to Seleucia and from there they sailed to Cyprus."* (Acts 13:1–4)

This gathering in Antioch is described as a church meeting that was comprised of a group that was spending intentional time "ministering" to the Lord and fasting. During this meeting, the Holy Spirit spoke to them and called out Barnabas and Saul (Paul) to be *set apart*. The Lord makes it clear that they are set apart for work. Their call to be set apart was a commission to be sent out as missionaries and church planters to unreached areas of the Roman empire. In being set apart by the Holy Spirit to be sent out, they entered into what we would term vocational ministry. They became part of a uniquely called element of the body of Christ that I like to refer to as the 3%. Paul's metron changed when he was set apart. He was not considered better or more holy than another believer, but he was called by God to work in full-time vocational ministry.

Notice that the church meeting that was happening in Antioch was filled with notable and spiritually gifted individuals who were actively ministering to the Lord. They were cultivating and keeping their metrons and managing the spiritual atmosphere of their garden. The description of this thriving church meeting is a benchmark for the level of spiritual activity that should be found in every metron. From this dynamic, active community of believers, the Holy Spirit selected some to serve as the 3%.

What then becomes of the 97% who are not called out to a full time, vocational ministry? Are they any less valued or less significant in the kingdom? I suggest that you are already called and set apart by the Lord to work in the metron to which God has assigned you. I believe we have made the case that everyone is given the same original commission to *cultivate* and *keep*. The 97% are equally called and commissioned, and they are no more and no less significant than the 3%.

The 97%

Within the body of Christ, the majority of believers are not called to a full-time traditional ministry role. We see in Paul's exhortation to the Thessalonians that most are called to work with their hands and excel in their vocations.

> "...But we urge you, brethren, to excel still more, and to make it your ambition to lead a quiet life and attend to your own business and work with your hands..."
> (1 Thessalonians 4:10b–11)

Those who are called to excel and attend to their own business and work with their hands are the 97%. Many in this majority demographic in the church would dismiss the Great Commission as irrelevant to their lives or metrons. Actually, the success of both the Great Commission and the Original Commission demand their full participation. No one is exempt from being on mission.

The 97% is called and positioned in their metrons to do the work of guarding, protecting, and watching over. This majority is commissioned to teach others how to manage their metron. The experience and understanding that they are amassing through the multifaceted or manifold wisdom of God have equipped them to teach others, to guard, protect, and watch over all of our father's interests. Qualitative work in the kingdom is as much a part of the Great Commission as the going, preaching, and baptizing.

When a member of the 97% is not called or compelled to emphasize the quantitative function, their obligation toward being on *mission* continues. This does not mean they are any less spiritual or that their work is any less meaningful than those who labor as part of the 3%. The quantitative and qualitative aspects are not mutually exclusive. The whole of each commission is given to each member of the body of Christ.

No two metrons look exactly the same, and no two metrons need exactly the same sort of redemptive labor. In managing your sphere of influence, the need for quantitative and qualitative work ebbs and flows.

Holistic Mission

3% + 97% = 100%

The Kingdom of God suffers from lost fruit and irrelevancy in the world because all "ministry" or "discipleship" is left up to the 3%. The principle at work is that everything reproduces after its own kind. This is why one often sees that a believer who is discipled by a "3%-er" will only think they are *discipled* or in obedience to Christ if they too go into full-time vocational ministry.

Many whose calling and metron lie within the 97% have forced their way into a full-time vocational ministry position based on a sense of guilt imparted to them by 3%-ers. Sadly many of these individuals do not thrive, and some become bitter and disillusioned. The irony is that when they drop out of *ministry* and return to working in the marketplace, they often return to the realm of influence to which they were originally called. Be sure, the sacred vs. secular gnostic deception will bear its fruit if accepted by a disciple.

> "*Therefore, since we receive a kingdom which cannot be shaken, let us show gratitude, by which we may offer to God an acceptable service with reverence and awe.*"
> (Hebrews 12:28)

All members of the body of Christ are instructed to offer God an acceptable service. The kingdom enterprise, or family business, is characterized by durability. The author of Hebrews clearly states that it cannot be shaken. Both elements of the Original and the Great Commissions are the means through which God has chosen to build his kingdom. God builds well, and he builds to last.

One of his revealed ways is that what he builds cannot be shaken. We should apply this idea of durability as we obey his instruction to teach obedience to all he has commanded. (Matthew 28) Who is best positioned to teach disciples that quality and durability are indicators of the *acceptable service* that is offered as worship? A faithful member of the body of Christ who has beheld this aspect of the character and nature of God and is committed to doing his will on earth as it is done in heaven.

This disciple has become like his father in that he builds with quality in mind. Some discipleship is best done by a member of the 97% — providing that the one doing the discipling understands their scriptural authority, power, and has a commission to do so.

The kingdom is durable by design; both expansion and durability are essential. The father's building code sets the standard. His standard is that what is built cannot be shaken.

What is the cost of marginalizing much of the 97%? If vocation is denigrated, and work is considered unspiritual those that could bring heavens solutions to the chaos and brokenness of creation often find themselves sitting out of the game. If the majority of the body of Christ view themselves as marginalized second class citizens in the kingdom, then there is little wonder that some metrons go unmanaged. Most metrons are marked by sin. They are messy, dynamic, and complex. We need the manifold wisdom of God in order to know how to manage these metrons. The required wisdom and understanding necessary for successful influence are spread throughout the body of Christ. The Bible says that *we* have the mind of Christ. God's design is that we would need each other and function as a well-coordinated body.

Together, as the body of Christ, we have the ability to see, think, and act like Christ. As great as our need is, God has provided for it. Those who resonate and excel in the 3% and those that resonate and excel in their vocations in the 97% each carry an aspect of the image of God. There are no holistic outcomes in the kingdom without complimentary gifts and labor working together.

Teaching the body of Christ to obey all that Christ has commanded requires *all to teach all*. The King is concerned about all that belongs to the King. God is concerned about the salvation of souls. He also knows that these souls must be taught to manage creation. Managing creation in a spiritually-minded way through holistic discipleship requires the hands-on teaching, modeling, and mentoring by the 97%. Each of us is commissioned to be expert at occupying through vocation.

Vocation is the platform where the ways of God are made known to the world, and heaven's software displaces the works of darkness. Hope finds a voice, and righteousness is championed in the context of vocation. The 97% burn with a desire to create, build, expand, improve, and steward. These compulsions are hard-coded in every believer by the creator. The desire to work is in line with the ways of God and validated through the original commission.

When pursuing these desires, we have the privilege of laboring alongside our father. In the context of your metron, you get to create, build, expand, improve, and steward. Answering the call to *abad* and *shamar* in your metron is not only permitted, but it is required in the Kingdom of God.

It is OK to be excited about your career! It is OK to embrace the vocation of parenting! It is OK to be passionate about creating solutions for government, arts, education, economics, family, science, and invention. You have permission and a commission to embrace and own your vocation! Innovation and creativity are part of your original design as an image-bearer of the Creator! All of these areas and many more are the vehicles through which *abad* and *shamar* operate in the Kingdom of God.

This practical theology is a call to action. Everyone is called to vocation, and everyone has a metron in which to manage the ways and presence of God and bring that light into every dark corner of creation. People are suffering and dying in the deserts of our metrons, and they desperately need the water of life to flow from heaven through you. Whether you resonate with the calling of the 3% in vocational ministry or with the 97% who's ministry is vocation, all are called and commissioned. All are on mission.

The 97% must see their identity and purpose clearly articulated when reading the Original and Great Commissions. Keeping the environment of your metron spiritually cultivated produces a culture that is attractive to the King. This is the aim of your stewardship—to align the ways that govern earth with the ways of heaven. The ways of God are the proper software that brings life to the hardware of creation. When led by the Spirit, your work is worship, and your vocation becomes *missionized*.

Missionized vocation is at the heart of kingdom expansion. Within every metron, there are outlying edges that have yet to encounter the Kingdom. These are what I would describe as missional edges in the Kingdom. As the Kingdom expands and your sphere of influence expands, you will increasingly encounter these rough edges. These edges are what attract the attention and focus of the missionized.

When God gave Adam and Eve the original commission, he built in a requirement for mission. God built the need for "mission" by leaving some things unfinished in the created order. Subdue, cultivate, and keep all imply a missional edge inherent in their meaning. Laboring alongside God to manage your metron requires an activated missional perspective.

Everyone's Mission

If you resonate as part of the 97%, let me ask you this question. Have you ever left a talk on missions feeling affirmed about your calling and vocation in the corporate world? Conversely, if you are clearly a member of the 3%, let me ask you this question. Have you ever left a mission conference excited about the work your friends are doing in the corporate world?

> *"But in fact God has placed the parts in the body, every one of them, just as he wanted them to be. If they were all one part, where would the body be? As it is, there are many parts, but one body. The eye cannot say to the hand, 'I don't need you!' And the head cannot say to the feet, 'I don't need you!'"* (1 Corinthians 12:18–12 NIV)

To help believers recognize the metron God has given them is a significant aspect of discipleship and is helping them to recognize God's calling. Each believer's metron is a dynamic ecosystem and is subject to change. This is why the experience, authority, and expertise of the 97% and the 3% are vital to a holistic discipleship process. Life in the kingdom truly is designed to function as an interdependent system. Every member of the Body of Christ is designed to be vital and useful. There are no unnecessary parts, and as Scripture says, we cannot say that we have no need for another part of the body.

Why do some resonate with the first element of the great commission yet gloss over the second? Humans customarily embrace what is understood. The first part of the Great Commission is easily understood and perceived as something that could be completed. Excessive focus on "completion" of the Great Commission may minimize or diminish the effort paid to second half of the commission. Some discontent about "teaching them to obey" all that Christ has commanded arises because it doesn't nicely fit into common theological paradigms.

Being aware of that, how do we actually *complete* this portion of the Great Commission? It may be that what we approached as a task may actually be more of a mandate. I believe that the heart of the Great Commission is pointing us toward a wide-open, bright, encouraging, and hope-filled future. To live in the kingdom is to experience a beautiful cycle of humans being born, coming into relationship with Christ, knowing and being known by God, learning and living all that Christ has commanded, then reproducing that in others and the world around us.

Is there a tendency in the church merely to reduce the Great Commission to a *task* that is to be completed at the earliest possible moment? Has this emphasis drained some of the beauty of life? Has the value of vocation been disparaged? Has much of creation been left without *shamar*? It may be that a fixation on completing only a quantitative task has produced a limited and lifeless product. If our Great Commission goals are limited to geographic technicalities or to a checklist of people groups, we may miss the beauty of the full kingdom process that God designed.

The dignity and purpose of the Body of Christ must be holistically championed. The work of the 3% and the 97% are equally valid in the commissions. Quantitative and qualitative results matter in the kingdom. Everyone's metron matters, and everyone is called to be on mission.

I have observed the continued frustration of the mission-minded 97%. These followers of Christ often feel that being involved in their metron is holding them back from having any means of obeying the Great Commission. If the idea of vocation as mission is minimized some believers, in turn, begin to denigrate the elements of their own metron.

They may feel trapped in what they view as secular, believing that their sphere of responsibility is *in the way* of doing something spiritual. When labor, work, or vocation is stripped of eternal value, people are not fulfilled in life, families suffer, and in the long run, they finally abdicate any sense of responsibility for the Great Commission.

I have felt this tension and sense of dissonance when sharing the command to reach the world with the Gospel of Christ. The gnostic or dualistic view that many Christians unintentionally embrace is crippling the potential of the 97%, and it impacts our mission sending efforts. If members of the body of Christ, those called to occupy and excel in their vocations, are devalued, they tend to feel condemned. This undue guilt often causes these vital stewards of the kingdom to turn their backs on the Great Commission. Sadly, they often receive no exhortation or empowerment to embrace the commissions and effectively manage their realms of influence.

Often when people who really do resonate with heaven, hear reports about full-time missionary work or full-time vocational ministry they are influenced by the sacred-secular divide in their thinking. Thinking that some activities are sacred and some are secular, they conclude that if I am not a pastor, church planter, cross cultural missionary or evangelist then I must be living in some degree of disobedience. Some may even feel that their career is some form of limitation that they must overcome — as if it were some lifestyle of sin. They sense very little validation or value being placed on those who are actually called to do the deep work of *shamar* and *abad* in the kingdom.

Many in the 97% are burning with a desire to see the kingdom come on earth as it is in heaven but feel side-lined as long as they continue to obey their call to a vocation. The work of *shamar* must be championed if the lives and callings of the 97% are to be validated. *Téreó* work must be held in high spiritual esteem alongside the quantitative efforts in the kingdom. Without a holistic understanding of mission, we will continue to see Great Commission progress bottlenecked. Nations and metrons continue to suffer under the prince of the power of air unless the works of darkness are displaced. If the 97% are fully empowered and championed to fulfill both elements in the commissions then the work of the 3% would accelerate, and the fruit would remain.

Missionized

The third element of vocation is all about becoming missionized. Mission-ized does not necessarily mean that everyone is called to become a voca-tional missionary. However, it does mean everyone is on mission by virtue of their vocation. How do we know if we are thinking holistically about the great commission and the original commission? Consider these key indicators that will help you evaluate your own beliefs and values regarding mission. These indicators are just that, indicators. They are not intended to answer every variable in missiology or give specific action steps. These indicators may help you evaluate if you are on mission as you manage your metron.

Key Indicators of the Missionized

1. *Abad* and *shamar* are considered of equal value.
2. Vocation is viewed as occupying.
3. The work done by the 97% is of equal value to the work of the 3%.
4. Qualitative and quantitative work are viewed as equal in the Great Commission
5. You have a non-binary understanding of Mission.
6. Those called as the 97% keep a holistic mentality about being on mission and involve themselves regularly with short and intermedi-ate-term assignments with the 3%.
7. The 3% actively involve the 97% in their ministry to help disciple, *cultivate*, and *keep*.
8. Both the 3% and the 97% recognize you reproduce after your own kind and that discipleship in the kingdom requires the involvement of all who are serving the King.
9. The 97% are not viewed as living in disobedience by answering the call to their vocation.
10. Those in the 97% are not viewed as second class citizens in the kingdom but as vital to reversing the effects of the fall in every metron.
11. Work is understood as eternal in nature and the means through which God has chosen to build his kingdom.
12. Work is understood as being established by God before the fall and is not a result of the fall.

13. Work is understood as the primary means of worshiping God and cultivating and keeping creation.
14. Work imparts dignity by design.
15. The missionized understand and embrace both elements of the Great Commission.
16. The missionized intentionally fill their metron with the atmosphere of heaven.
17. The missionized understand that everything is spiritual, and there is no false, gnostic delineation between sacred and secular.
18. The missionized understand that everything done in obedience is worship, and worship is sacred.
19. The missionized expect and embrace expansion in their metron.
20. The 97% realize that they cannot opt-out of their role in the Original and Great Commissions.
21. *Shamar* style work is championed as complementary and equal to the quantitative work of evangelism, church planting, and traditional vocational ministry activities.
22. Quality assurance is viewed as being on mission.
23. The 97% embrace their role to diligently watch over the condition of their metron—like a hawk that circles its territory.
24. The missionized make disciples who *abad* and *shamar* in the kingdom.
25. The missionized recognize that the presence of God radiates from what is subdued.
26. The missionized bear fruit and are a blessing to all of creation.
27. The missionized create an atmosphere in their metron that is welcoming and attractive to the presence of God. The King feels like he is right at home when he visits their garden.
28. The missionized actively steward their connection point with God and manage external realities according to the inner reality shaped by relationship with God.
29. The missionized always align their metron with God's ways. They live from heaven towards the earth and embrace the calling to co-labor with God to manage their metron toward fulfilling Jesus' prayer—on earth as it is in heaven.

Qualified for Mission

You might be asking yourself, "Am I qualified to live on mission in my metron?" I believe scripture makes it clear that it is God who qualifies the called. He does not always call the qualified. Living "on mission" is simply doing what you can, when you can, where you can as a faithful co-laborer with Christ. It is simply valuing what God values and doing what he would do.

The way that one stays confident in their commission is to remember not only that we are saved from something we are saved to something. We are seated in heavenly places with Christ Jesus. Christ is seated at the right hand of God in his throne room. You are well-positioned and well-favored. If you are to live on mission in your metron, remember you live from heaven towards earth. You can allow freedom, joy, and peace to define you. Remember, you are not working *for favor* but working *from a place of favor*. You may feel unqualified to work in the kingdom, but Scripture tells us that it is God who qualifies you. The apostle Paul made this abundantly clear in Colossians 1:12–13 when he said, "...and giving joyful thanks to the Father, who has qualified you to share in the inheritance of his holy people in the kingdom of light. For he has rescued us from the dominion of darkness and brought us into the kingdom of the Son he loves." (NIV) You are qualified because you are saved and positioned in Christ's kingdom. You have received the necessary authority, mandate, and plan from God to manage your realm. You are qualified to live on the missional edge in your metron.

The Missional Edge

The plans and purposes of God for his creation start with the free offer of salvation. God wants all men to be redeemed and reconciled to him, and he has done everything possible to prevent mankind from spending eternity outside the kingdom. God sent his only son to pay the cost of restoring us to our original position as a vice-regents. We are those to whom is given authority, mandates, and means to oversee his creation.

Looking at the redemptive meta-narrative in scripture, we see that his goal has been "his kingdom come and his will be done" from the very beginning. Through the work of Jesus Christ, the kingdom is not only established but is now unstoppable. The prophet Isaiah famously prophesied about the nature of the coming Kingdom of Heaven.

He said, in Isaiah 9:6–7, "For a child will be born to us, a son will be given to us; And the government will rest on his shoulders; And his name will be called Wonderful Counselor, Mighty God, Eternal Father, Prince of Peace. There will be no end to the increase of his government or of peace."

As Christ's Kingdom advances, unkept, uncultivated edges are increasingly exposed in every metron. These edges are sin, evil desires, evil designs, corruption, and chaos manifest throughout creation. The more that is added to the kingdom, the more these missional edges must be addressed. You, as the cultural apostle to your metron, or *metron apostle*, are commissioned to find those rough edges and work to reverse the effects of the fall. There are missional edges visible at any time you look around and honestly evaluate the condition of your metron.

The spiritual and natural condition of mankind and all of creation is desperate for a touch from heaven. These edges are not to be ignored as these are the very focus of mission in your metron. Missional edges could be described as anything that is operating with the wrong source code. These edges become obvious because they are incompatible with the ways of God. When seen in comparison to his character and nature, the broken conditions become obvious. Broken edges result from the willing alignment of sinful man and rebellious, evil forces that have attempted to assert themselves against the one true Living God. The enemy does fulfill his aim to kill, steal and destroy. The gardens that he has been allowed to rule are filled with snakes and weeds.

Restoring the broken edges in nations, cultures, lives, and souls is the business of the metron apostle. The restoration of all things through reconciliation with Christ is the undercurrent of activity within every metron. Cultivating and keeping is the mandate, and subduing is the mission. The mission of subduing the broken edges in your metron requires the diligent work of *shamar*. Attention to the qualitative condition of your metron is an indicator that you are Missionized and holistically obeying the original and great commission.

Chapter 25

Managing Expansion

IN SCRIPTURE, WE ARE PRESENTED WITH A vision of human history that has an opening sequence in the garden and a concluding sequence of a garden city descending from heaven to earth. Much has happened and will continue to happen between these two scenes in the Bible.

There is no allowance for passive metron managers. Just as everyone is given a calling and a metron, everyone is given a commission *to mission*. Your life and work are vital building blocks in God's kingdom project, and this project is not stagnant. As history is unfolding, the kingdom is also advancing. The new territory will constantly present itself within your metron. This new territory requires subjugation, and God is entrusting you to cultivate and keep it.

Expansion is Obedience

"Enlarge the place of your tent, stretch your tent curtains wide, do not hold back; lengthen your cords, strengthen your stakes. For you will spread out to the right and to the left; your descendants will dispossess nations and settle in their desolate cities." (Isaiah 54:2–3 NIV)

Enlarge your place, expand your footprint, set up longer ropes and stronger stakes! Does this sound familiar? Everyone in the Kingdom of God is commissioned to spread out, fill the earth, and subdue it. As Isaiah prophecies, you will dispossess nations and settle in empty places. You will occupy. Your metron will be defined by both the quantitative and the qualitative aspects of expansion. You are to enlarge your place and strengthen your stakes. You are to spread out and settle what is desolate.

Expansion is not to be feared. Rather, it is to be embraced. The increase is evidence that the kingdom is here and yet still coming. Throughout scripture, the recurring theme of expansion and increase presented in a positive light. In fact, it is the very nature of the Kingdom of God. Here are a few passages that express the expansive design of God's purposes for creation.

> *"His rule will extend from sea to sea and from the river to the ends of the earth."* (Zechariah 9:10)
> *"...For the earth will be full of the knowledge of the LORD ... As the waters cover the sea."* (Isaiah 11:9b)
> *"There will be no end to the increase of his government or of peace."* (Isaiah 9:7a)
> *"Go therefore and make disciples of all the nations..."* (Matthew 28:19a)

Expansion and increase are inherent dynamics in the Kingdom of God. Managing expansion is part of the job description for metron managers. Managing expansion is the essence of being on mission. Expansion creates new challenges and new opportunities. Being on mission or missional is both a mentality and an activity that all believers are called to. This missional mentality could be described as a spiritual scanning system that operates primarily as discernment. One who is spiritually minded and has the mentality of being on mission is constantly assessing the metron environment, looking for anything that is out of alignment with the ways of God. The spiritually-minded believer not only has a mentality of being on mission but translates their findings into action. Taking action is to co-labor with God in the work of redemption and reconciliation. With the apostle Paul, we affirm that the universal call for believers is to do the work of reconciliation.

Reconciliation

> *"Now all these things are from God, who reconciled us to himself through Christ and gave us the ministry of reconciliation."* (2nd Corinthians 5:18)

The word *reconciliation* carries two primary meanings. One is the idea of restoring a relationship that was broken, but the other is the idea of alignment. A dictionary defines it as "the action of making one view or belief compatible with another."

This second definition is exactly what we are talking about when using the term *managing your metron*. Reconciliation is the missional work of every believer. It is the activity that defines whatever occupation to which you are called. You are commissioned to take action by discipling the views and beliefs of heaven into your metron. What are views and beliefs other than the foundations of culture? Kingdom culture is a culture that has views and beliefs compatible with the Kingdom of God. *Abad*, *shamar*, and *occupy* are all missional because they all are intended to accomplish reconciliation between God and Man. Do not discount or denigrate the work of reconciliation. Under the new covenant, reconciliation is the goal of both the Original and Great Commissions.

A garden that by nature grows but is left to the weeds, foxes, and foes represents *unmanaged expansion*. Uncultivated and unkempt gardens are the reality in most of the metrons of men. Culture is largely informed by the chaos and counterfeit claims that are allowed to thrive in such gardens.

People often feel responsible but powerless about the dynamics at work in their metron. It is normal to feel that things are getting away from you and that you are unable to keep up with the change that is all around. The harder things become the more meaningful opportunity you have to connect with the Lord. From personal connection with God come the love, wisdom, and power that are required to manage your metron towards the Kingdom of God. He has manifold answers to the manifold problems and questions that seem to overwhelm us in day to day life.

Through your personal relationship with God, you are given access to the manifold wisdom of God as the scripture indicates in Ephesians 3:10. The wisdom of God and combined with his gentle ways are the source code of heaven. God does not intend for us to feel confident in our own strength. The insight you need comes from pressing into him. He wants to manifest his ways through you. The outcomes bring him Glory. Every challenge encountered in your metron can be met with an answer from God. No challenge or need is beyond his solutions. He has your best in mind, and his intention is to bless you and all the nations of creation.

His original design is that the blessing comes through his co-laboring with you. This working relationship is how testimonies are born. When we testify to all that God has done in us, through us, and for us, we create an atmosphere of hope that attracts the lost. People have a built-in longing for a relationship with the divine. Even those within your metron who have never heard of God or the saving work of Christ are constantly aware that they were created for something more. This built-in sense of longing is answered when they hear your testimony and see you truly co-laboring with your Father God.

When a metron is managed in the manner we have discussed, the observer will realize that you could not do this on your own. The wisdom you have access to, the hope you have in the face of hardships, the love you have for the unlovable, the atmosphere of heaven that permeates your garden is good news to the lost. The gospel is more than the message of personal salvation. It is the message of hope for the nations and hope for all of creation.

An atmosphere that is filled with hope and restoration is the very aroma of Christ. Everyone has a longing, often unrecognized, for such hope. Much of our missional work is to expose people to the atmosphere of heaven—the order and beauty that is available in the Kingdom of God. Christ is prophetically referred to as the "Desire of all Nations" in Haggai 2:7. The metron that is managed from heaven towards earth will attract the lost. If people experience the kingdom, they will want to meet the king.

It is the nature of the family business that things are constantly changing. It is expanding. God is constantly at work, and we are constantly trying to keep up! If we are going to be found faithful with our father's possessions and interests, we have to focus on managing expansion.

Now that we have explored the original commission and the Great Commission, it becomes clear that all are called to be on mission. What sort of mission is a believer engaged in when managing their metron? There is the obvious quantitative work of reaching lost souls and subduing the work of darkness in creation. But what about the command to tend and keep? How is one on mission if their primary activity is one who guards, protects, and watches over? What exactly are you watching over? Psalm 67 provides an insight into the broader work of mission. The qualitative work of the Kingdom is to guard what culture is established on the earth.

"May God be gracious to us and bless us and make his face shine on us—so that your ways may be known on earth, your salvation among all nations." (Psalm 67:1–2)

Those who *keep* are guarding, protecting, and watching over the ways of God. Remember the source code that informs a culture can be described as ways. God's ultimate aim is that his *ways* may be known on the earth. It is the devil's ultimate aim that God's ways would be supplanted by the counterfeit source code of darkness. The missional work of keeping is to identify when, where and how the enemy is attempting a move towards moral equivalency with God and then expose the schemes of the devil. The enemy's prideful and counterfeit ways must not go unchallenged.

The salvation of the nations is at stake when God's ways are not made known on the earth. The outcome of God's ways being made known on the earth is that salvation happens among the nations. This is the Gospel. This is *good news*. The ways of God are good news, and salvation is the result. The Gospel was originally announced to Abraham as a *blessing*. God told Abraham I will bless you, and you will be a blessing.

Psalm 67 leads us to ask for this—"May God be gracious to us and bless us…" so that God's ways would be made known, and *salvation* would be made known among the lost, among the nations. The qualitative mission is to make known God's ways in your metron. If the ways of God are not made known on earth, the nations will not find salvation. Mission is as much about cultivating and keeping the ways of God front and center in your metron as it is about evangelism or church planting.

Guard and Protect

Being on mission in your metron is all about guarding and protecting your sphere of influence from the ways of the enemy. Your mission is to cultivate and keep the source code of heaven flowing into every dimension of your metron.

The one who will be trusted as a kingdom Influencer is the one who knows the ways of God, not just his acts. Moses is an example of one who was trusted and knew the ways of God.

"The Lord would speak to Moses face to face, as one speaks to a friend." (Exodus 33:11 NIV)

How did Moses get to know the ways of God? He asked God to teach him. Moses continued to pray, "If you are pleased with me, teach me your ways so I may know you and continue to find favor with you." (Exodus 33:13a)

In Psalm 103, David is musing on the ways of God, and he recounts the distinction between Moses and the nation of Israel. In verse seven, he wrote, "He made known his *ways* to Moses, his *acts* to the sons of Israel." (emphasis added)

God's activities are visible to all. But understanding his ways comes from a place of trusted, intimate relationship with him. Moses had this type of relationship. Abraham also was called the friend of God. Now in the New Covenant, you are taught the ways of God by the Holy Spirit. Access to the manifold wisdom of God is promised to you as a member of the Body of Christ. Paul wrote in Ephesians 3:10 that through the Church the many-faceted, i.e., manifold, wisdom of God will be made known to spiritual authorities who want to assert their ways over and above the ways of God. This is the true culture war, and this war is fought at the highest levels.

The world around you will look like the world inside you, and you will resemble what you revere. The transformed metron has been leavened by the presence of God. When his presence and his ways are manifest in your metron, it will be a witness to the nations.

Today, in the new covenant, the presence of God is what distinguishes the people of God. When God is recognized and worshiped, his ways are showcased for all to see. When the ways of God are manifest, this distinguishes a discipled individual and a well-managed metron in the kingdom. Springs of living water in a dry and weary land are not easily rejected by those who wander in the desert.

The Great Commission is great for a number of reasons. One particular reason is that God is saying, "I trust you." Nothing motivates a person more than being trusted. Jesus is entrusting us with authority and sends us to take the Holy Spirit to places where his ways are not yet known. The Good News, or *gospel*, is that through you, God is re-introducing his presence into the chaos of rebellious creation. Salvation is here, and the kingdom is at hand. Within the world, there are countless areas that are unreached by the Gospel, and within your metron there are countless areas that have not been subdued by the King. On the cross Jesus said, "It (his work) is finished" but at the Great Commission he said you are just getting started. God gave mankind the keys to the kingdom, and mankind gave them to the adversary. Jesus took them back from Satan and returned them to mankind.

In your metron, it is likely, many snakes remain. The "ruler of this world" is still viciously asserting his claims over God's creation. Even though he was outmaneuvered by Jesus and lost his authority, he has not lost his motivation. He continues still to kill, steal, and destroy. If the enemy can deceive you into lending him your strength and convincing you to align with his ways then he expands his business. Although it is a temporary arrangement he can still cause tremendous damage.

The enemy knows that you are on mission to reverse the effects of the fall, and he will actively attempt to reimpose the effects of the fall. No backyard garden will remain cultivated and fruitful unless it is kept and tended. The same principle is at work in the life of those who are converted.

This is why the Great Commission mandates that we make disciples and not just converts. Remember that the condition of your metron is an outworking of your innermost being. Theologian GK Beal wrote, "You resemble what you revere." We were designed to revere God and by doing so, "heavenize" our hearts and metrons. But if you revere and obey the snake then do not be surprised when thorns spring up around you.

"For he must reign until he has put all his enemies under his feet." (1 Corinthians 15:25)

When Jesus died and then rose from the dead, he hit the reset button on his operating system. Your conversion and salvation became the starting point. Co-laboring in the kingdom became your sacred trust. There are great joy and adventure found in living, fighting, and working alongside Christ to establish his kingdom. Jesus outsmarted the devil and reset the game. Now all who follow Christ inherit a metron to manage. Every believer is in the game. Every believer is commissioned with responsibility. No one is exempt from playing their position in this season of *waiting*. Salvation reset your position with God and the Great Commission reset your purpose.

With your new identity in the kingdom, you can confidently look around your metron and discern what is not of heaven and work towards reversing the effects of the fall. This may seem like an overwhelming responsibility, but in truth, it is not. Remember you are co-laboring with

Christ and you are supernaturally empowered by the Holy Spirit. The wisdom you need is not in short supply, and God will give it to those who ask. God's ways, manifest as wisdom, flowing into creation through the church, will reprogram broken and desperate metrons.

Jesus refers to both the *Gospel of Salvation* and the *Gospel of the Kingdom*. The gospel of the kingdom is the holistic goal of Christ's work. It is reconciliation with mankind and the restoration of the created order, recovering its original design. The good news for your metron is that you are a conduit of hope. You are a conduit from heaven and conduct water to the deserts of earth. There is hope for the personal salvation of the lost, and there is hope for the restoration of all things. When Jesus commissioned his followers, he concludes his command by saying, "And surely I am with you always, to the very end of the age." (Matthew 28:20b)

Jesus reassures his disciples in giving them the Great Commission by saying he would be with them always. He recognizes that the temptation to be overwhelmed will be strong. He adds encouragement to assure them that what he commanded, he would make possible and he would be with them in this kingdom enterprise.

Conclusion

GOD HAS CALLED YOU TO A PARTICULAR vocation in a specific season in spiritual history. He has given you the tools to cultivate and keep all of his interests. You are commissioned to cultivate his ways into creation and guard, protect and watch over all that belongs to your Father. When you live from heaven towards earth, your metron will never be the same.

"Nations will come to your light, and kings to the brightness of your dawn." (Isaiah 60:3)

Isaiah said nations would be attracted to the brightness of the dawning Kingdom of God.

You are designed to exude the very manifest presence of God, and if the kingdom is visible in you, people will be attracted. When people fall in love with the Kingdom, they want to meet the King. Jesus is irresistible to the hungry and weary world.

Christ will return and complete the full restoration of all things. Here and now you are the one he has chosen to work through. Now is the time that the reconciled in Christ will bring restoration. You are a mobile temple that carries the presence of God, so let the rivers of living water flow!

Don't dream of the day you get to do something spiritually significant. No royal priest should ever say that "once I can get free of this job, then I can do something for the Lord." You are in the kingdom now, and the kingdom is trying to burst out of you and bring life to all that is around us.

Managing your metron requires you to remember that everything is spiritual and should refrain from living as a Christian gnostic. If you separate your spiritual life from your role in creation, the enemy will own what you don't occupy. True vocational success is to view everything you do, great and small, as an opportunity to worship God. Heaven longs to touch earth through you. When you live from heaven towards earth, there is hope for all of creation. When you manage your metron, God will be glorified through you, and many will find their way home. Manage your metron like it matters today, for tomorrow Jesus will meet you on the job.

Go manage your metron!

CPSIA information can be obtained
at www.ICGtesting.com
Printed in the USA
BVHW041441071020
590506BV00005B/263